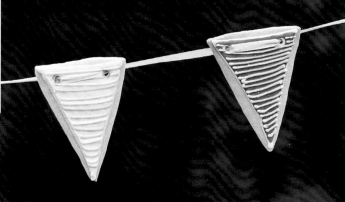

THE GREAT BRITISH
BAKING SHOW

LOVE TO BAKE

sphere

Contents

A Note from Paul

These have been difficult and challenging times for everyone, but we have done what we do best in a crisis and that's come together as a community. I have been truly humbled by stories of how communities have rallied to support neighbours, the elderly, the vulnerable, our key workers and the incredible NHS staff working on the frontline of this pandemic. Whether it be shopping, cooking, making a call to someone who is lonely, sewing face coverings and scrubs, or picking up prescriptions, people have found their own way to help and look out for each other.

For me, it has been wonderful to see how so many people have used baking as a way to lift spirits, teach and entertain children, and help the community – some baking for the first time, others using the enforced time at home to revisit a long-forgotten passion, all united in wanting to feed and share. Even when there was a great big flour-shaped hole on shops' shelves, seeing how innovative people were in their baking was really inspiring.

It is those favourite, go-to or special bakes that bring comfort and a smile. I think the recipes in this book really reflect that spirit and are perfect for baking for and baking with others. Our fabulous bakers have shared their own favourite recipes, feel-good bakes made with love. There are recipes from Prue and me and the *Bake Off* team – great for challenging your own baking skills.

As we ease out of lockdown, reunite with family and friends and embark on the 'new normal', let's celebrate the simple pleasures in life that have shone a light during these darker times. And I can think of no better way than with a cup of tea and a slice of cake or freshly baked loaf.

A Note from Prue

One of life's greatest joys is feeding people. It doesn't need to be fancy or expensive. The simple act of making really delicious food to share is what I love. I have always been a feeder – my husband used to say I got almost as much pleasure out of feeding the horses hot bran and carrots and the chickens leftover scraps, as I did out of cooking for the family.

But over the years, what with running a business and writing novels, I had baked less and less. *Bake Off* changed that. Inspired by the talented team who make the show, and our incredible bakers who manage to bring something new to the tent year on year, I started stealing their recipes to bake at home. Passion re-ignited, I'm now as enthusiastic a baker as ever.

Lockdown has been an anxious time, separating me from my children and grandchildren; worrying about the impact on business, the NHS, friends and colleagues. But I'm also aware how lucky I've been. Lockdown has afforded me the luxury of time at home, not working, and time to spend with my husband, take stock, be still, walk the dogs, appreciate the garden and perfect the Paul Hollywood brioche a tête!

Baking is such a great way to share food, celebrate events, thank people and show them you care. Each week I baked Friday night supper for the staff at our local care home. It was a great excuse to bake, and to do those old-fashioned dishes that spell comfort and love: chicken pies and pasta bakes, and (of course) pastries and cakes. I wish I'd had this book then – it is full of recipes for sharing, but also ideas that are perfect for gifts, picnics, baking with children, or feeding the family.

Bake Off is a global community, bringing people together physically and virtually and it is a privilege to be part of that. When people talk to me about the show, they often mention the kindness that runs through it. They love seeing the bakers helping each other, forgetting that they are rivals. They can tell we are all – presenters, judges, crew and bakers – having a happy time. And most of all they tell me that this year, more than ever before, they value that sense of community, the camaraderie, and the obvious pleasure the bakers have in doing what they love. I do think *Bake Off* is a force for good, and never more needed and valued than it has been this year.

Introduction

Welcome to *The Great British Bake Off: Love to Bake*, a collection of sweet and savoury bakes from Paul, Prue and the team behind the show – as well, of course, as from our wonderful 2020 bakers themselves.

When we first thought about the concept for this book, the notion of 'love to bake' seemed a way to express all the many guises and reasons that we head to the kitchen in search of butter, sugar, eggs and flour. From baking as a fun activity with the kids, through rustling up bakes for an office cake sale, conjuring up a showstopper of a birthday cake, or creating something heavenly to round off a dinner party, to baking just because it makes us feel better (who doesn't find kneading dough or turning egg whites into cloudy meringue therapeutic?), the book was to be a collection of recipes that would capture the sense of community, belonging, love and well-being that has become more-or-less synonymous with baking. We have always known that baking is an important feature in many people's lives, but we could never have imagined just how significant this humble pastime would become for life in 2020.

This year, most of us have spent more time in our homes than we ever imagined we would. And, for many of us, that has also meant spending more time in our kitchens, hands covered in flour, surfaces sticky with buttercream and ovens pumping out the mouthwatering smells of our toils. When the notion of 'lockdown' hit our world, the baking staples were among the first to fly off the supermarket shelves (after toilet roll, that is, and somewhere around the same time as pasta). Flour, caster sugar, eggs, yeast... became precious, hard-to-come-by commodities. At the supermarkets, instead of myriad sugars and a gazillion types of flour, the baking aisles were oddly bare. When we managed to secure what we needed, we shared photos of ourselves on our doorsteps with our best efforts, and we delivered treats to those who weren't able to get out of the house themselves. Offering to leave a neighbour a portion of bread flour at their front door became an act of kindness almost as comforting as the loaf of bread itself.

Suddenly, then, the notion of 'love to bake' seemed so much more significant than it had been way back when we first sat around a meeting-room table (together, actually in an office, no screens involved) and talked about what baking really means to us all and how we could reflect that in this year's *Great British Bake Off* book.

So, whether by accident or by design, *Love to Bake* is a book that captures the true spirit of baking – the very (vanilla) essence that had us all stripping the baking shelves bare at the start of lockdown. This book is about baking for ourselves, with our loved ones and for our friends, family and the community around us, in kindness, togetherness and celebration.

Whether you are baking to pass the time, to relax or to have fun in the kitchen, or whether baking is a way to tell someone that you care, this book is packed with recipes intended to sprinkle joy near and far. Some of those recipes are quick and easy (and no less enticing for it), some will stretch you to achieve perhaps more than you thought possible, many will have you licking the spoon in impatient anticipation, and when things eventually get back to normal, plenty are sure to win you the coveted first prize in your street's community bake off. With all that in mind, and with love – happy baking!

USING THIS BOOK

The book is divided into six recipe chapters, each focusing on a way in which baking demonstrates love for others and even for ourselves.

Acts of Kindness is a collection of recipes that are perfect for baking for other people – either as a gift (perhaps a thank you, a congratulations, or a get well soon), or a simple 'I love you'. Many are easy to parcel up in pretty boxes and tie with string or ribbon to deliver to a friend or neighbour in need. Bakes such as the Sticky Toffee Puddings on page 50 are easily freezable – what could be lovelier than having a treat delivered to enjoy today, and then to enjoy next week, too? Special mention must go to the dog biscuits on page 63. What better way to say thank you to man and woman's best friend than wholesome, homemade treats? We invite you to raise a paw.

We couldn't create a book about the love of baking without including a chapter intended for **Little Bakers**. Apart from it being in our best interests to encourage and inspire the next generation of *Bake Off* contestants, baking with children is a way to bring families together in the kitchen. Weighing, measuring, and being precise about methods and techniques are all forms of home-schooling that definitely don't feel like school at all – especially when you get to cover the results in sprinkles and eat them. From the classic Butterfly Cakes on page 92 through a simple foray into the world of meringues on page 79 to Paul's Rainbow-coloured Bagels (see p.81), the chapter brims with sweet (and savoury) family treats to make and enjoy together.

From there to **Celebrate** – because creating something for a special occasion is the ultimate way to show people you care. Here, find bakes for festivals and occasions, from Christmas to Diwali, and birthday cakes and party bakes to fill a room with oohs and aahs. Best of all is a gorgeous wedding cake (see p.113), a two-tiered, double-flavoured stunner of a cake that is straightforward enough to make at home even the day before the big event. It belies its simple roots in its glorious presentation, decorated as it is with beautiful fresh flowers.

Just Because is a chapter dedicated to bakes that are therapeutic in some way – either because they offer a kind of self-comfort (think Chicken and Leek Pie on page 159 with a buttery, flaky crust and warming, flavourful filling; or Cinnamon and Apple Buns that are just heavenly with a cup of tea), trigger a memory, or involve techniques that will stretch your skills and encourage you to experiment to find out what baking wizardry you're really capable of. This is baking for well-being, personal fulfilment and self-care – comfort-baking at its best.

From cake sales to charity bake offs, and summer fêtes to an office birthday, the recipes in **Community** are easy wins when you are setting up a stall or trying to feed a crowd. This chapter is where you'll find delicious traybakes such as Speculoos Cheesecake Squares (see p.224), pretty individual cupcakes such as the vegan Sticky Toffee Apple Cakes (see p.217), and Paul's Jam and Custard Doughnuts (see p.201) – a certain hit at any charity coffee morning. And, if you're looking to offer some doorstep sandwiches at your community event, be sure to make them with homemade sourdough (see p.219).

The book closes with a chapter on **Gatherings**. These are the bakes that wow your guests around a lunch or dinner table, from nibbles, through mains to desserts – including an irresistible Basque Cheesecake (see p.246; even those who say they don't like cheesecake have been known to ask for a second slice) and spectacular, towering Croquembouche (see p.255). And, of course, no chapter intended to provide desserts for a dinner party would be complete without a pavlova – this one in the form of Fig, Pomegranate and Cardamom Pavlova (see p.261), to give a North African twist on the strawberries-and-cream classic.

Throughout the book there are free-from bakes to please everyone, including dairy-free gluten-free and vegan cakes and savouries. Keep an eye out for the symbols at the bottom of the ingredients' lists to indicate where recipes are suitable for certain diets. At the end of the book you can find a full list of these bakes grouped together, as well as a list of the vegetarian savoury bakes that appear in the book.

Finally, at the beginning and end of the book are baking essentials – starting with the things you'll need in your kitchen (and some you don't need, but are useful to have) and ending with some of the key tips and techniques to give your bakes the professional results worthy of any *Bake Off* contestant.

Of course, there are many recipes that could just as easily find their way into another chapter, so if you find something in Little Bakers that you want to serve up at a dinner party, go ahead! If you think the wedding cake would make the perfect celebration cake for a relative's birthday, who needs a bride and groom? At the end of the book, as well as a standard index, we've provided a thematic index to group together the recipes according to their type. We hope this will inspire you to use the book creatively – to explore your own baking journey in as many fun and fulfilling ways as possible.

DAVE, 30
HAMPSHIRE
Armoured Guard

As a child, Dave rarely ventured into the kitchen to cook, relying entirely on his mum's cooking – he taught himself to bake only once he'd flown the nest. Now living with his girlfriend in their first home, he loves filling his kitchen with fancy, colourful gadgets and he even chooses his appliances with *Bake Off* in mind! Dave bakes at least once a week – and always while listening to his favourite punk rock bands. His baking style is innovative and imaginative and his strengths lie in bread (pretzels, brioche rolls, and baguettes are particular favourites) and decoration – he especially loves a mirror glaze to give his bakes a professional-looking finish. When he's not baking, Dave can be found pursuing his other passions – cars, DIY, and taking his dog and cat for walks.

HERMINE, 38
LONDON
Accountant

Hermine was born and raised in Benin, West Africa, and moved to London in 2001 to pursue further education. Growing up, she used to love helping her mum bake for big family gatherings, and then at the age of eight decided to go about it on her own. She bought the ingredients for a Savarin cake and threw herself into the challenge. She has never looked back! The French influence in Benin has instilled in Hermine a love of high-end pâtissérie – she enjoys baking intricate millefeuille, éclairs and entremets. She is also a dab hand at sourdough – so much so that her nine-year-old son now refuses to eat any other bread! A notorious feeder with an infectious laugh, she's creative at heart and loves cooking marmalades and jams to give as gifts, making beautiful labels as well as delicious fillings for the jars.

LAURA, 30
KENT
Digital Manager

A Gravesend girl born and bred, Laura began baking at around the age of eight but realised her flair for it only a few years ago. She loves citrus and strong flavours, and enjoys putting a modern twist on old classics. Laura thrives working under pressure and thinks her organised nature is what particularly suited her to taking part in *Bake Off*. The perfectionist in her wants things to look faultlessly pretty and gorgeously dainty. She specialises in decoration and is proud to have mastered the art of piped buttercream flowers. Laura is happily married to a Police Community Support Officer, and she loves musical theatre (as a performer and audience member) and is a volunteer for a charity helpline.

LINDA, 61
EAST SUSSEX
Retirement Living Team Leader

Linda discovered her passion for baking during her frequent childhood visits to her aunt's dairy farm, just down the road from her own home. She'd help to milk the cows, then carry a bucket of milk into the kitchen, where her aunt taught her to bake cakes topped with rich, creamy icing. To this day Linda buys homegrown produce from another aunt's fruit farm and uses it in her baking. Her strengths are in the classics and in home-comfort cooking, like her signature sausage rolls. A lover of the countryside and of being outdoors in general, Linda will frequently head with her partner to their local beach, to fish for mackerel and mullet. And she loves to spend time in her garden – cultivating its produce and for its positive effects on her well-being.

LORIEA, 27
DURHAM
Diagnostic Radiographer

Born and raised in Jamaica, Loriea uses baking as a means to celebrate her Caribbean roots. She moved to the UK when she was 15 years old, but began baking at age five with her maternal grandmother, whose influence plays a big part in her cooking style. Loriea loves to include coconut, chillies and cinnamon in her food – and rarely follows a recipe exactly. In fact, from the moment she reads a recipe, she starts to think how she can tweak it to make it her own. Her husband, Peter, is (of course) the biggest fan of her cooking, and he especially loves her Jamaican patties. When Loriea isn't baking or working long shifts at the hospital as a radiographer, she likes practising the craft of macramé. Growing up, Loriea was really into athletics – and has even met Usain Bolt.

LOTTIE, 31
WEST SUSSEX
Pantomime Producer

Lottie's Lancastrian great-grandmother was a fervent cake-baker – and for this reason Lottie believes that baking is in her blood. She has always had a fascination with cooking: when she was little, she watched cooking shows rather than playing with her toys and was often to be found making notes from cookery books. She calls herself a 'perpetually frustrated perfectionist' and, while her baking has become more refined over time, she hopes it retains an element of her dark sense of humour. When she's not baking or busy with her job producing pantomime, Lottie will be playing computer games with her young cousins, or practising yoga.

MAKBUL, 50
GREATER MANCHESTER
Accountant

Self-taught baker Makbul first took on cooking at home as a means to help support his mum. He has honed those early skills through watching TV shows, reading books and drawing inspiration from famous chefs. He has a remarkable ability to measure out ingredients just by eye. Mak's strengths lie in pastry (he says he's better at puff than shortcrust); and, for celebrations such as Eid, he enjoys making traditional Asian *nankhatai* biscuits. He thinks baking has made him generally more patient, but woe betide anyone (even his wife) who tries to take control in his kitchen! Their three grown-up children are his harshest baking critics. Mak has recently taken up beekeeping – he produces his own honey, which he loves to use as often as possible in his bakes.

MARC, 50
CORNWALL
Bronze Resin Sculptor

Marc decided to enter *Bake Off* in a bid to show his daughters that even when life throws obstacles at you, you can rise to new challenges and develop new passions. Born and raised in Leicester, fervent climber Marc spent his youth travelling the world and conquering mountains, before settling back in the UK and becoming a landscape photographer. Personal tragedy, including losing his leg in a motorbike accident in 2016, led him to baking bread as a form of therapy, and from there he came to baking cakes and pastries. From palmiers and chausson aux pommes to opera cakes and millefeuille, his bakes now show true finesse. He's a support worker and single parent, and, with his daughters to cheer him on, he's taken up climbing again.

MARK, 31
LIVERPOOL
Project Manager

Northern Irish Mark fell in love with baking at a pie shop in Edinburgh – he visited every day while he was at university for the shop's delicious Mac 'n' Cheese pie. Following that early inspiration, he began to experiment: first attempting (and perfecting) a lemon drizzle cake and eventually taking on multi-tiered wedding cakes, each time looking at the science of the bake in order to perfect it. His style is hugely influenced by his Irish heritage, but also by the flavours of Africa and Asia, where he travels regularly for his work as a project manager for public health research programmes. When he isn't baking, you can find Mark walking in the Lake District, indulging his passion for wildlife, or with his wife, travelling and exploring new places.

PETER, 19
EDINBURGH
Accounting &
Finance Student

With his parents and brother, Edinburgh-born Peter grew up feasting on his mum's home cooking. But it was *Bake Off* that inspired him to start baking for himself – he has watched every series since the first and has been baking seriously since he was only 12 years old. He loves to honour his homeland in his cooking, using Scottish ingredients – including berries, whisky, oats and honey – whenever he can. When he's not baking, he is either upholding the family's love of numbers by studying Accounting and Finance at university, or demonstrating his competitive streak on the badminton court – he has been playing badminton for a decade and has represented his county in the sport since 2012.

ROWAN, 54
WORCESTERSHIRE
Music Teacher

Entirely self-taught, Rowan calls his baking style ostentatious – but, he hopes, tasteful. French pâtissérie is his absolute passion – he loves the subtlety of flavour, and the style and sophistication of French baking, and he is drawn to fine, complex, layered cakes. His love of the Georgian era encourages him to reinvent 18th-century recipes whenever he can. He enjoys decorating his bakes with flowers, preferably edible ones, using what is in bloom in his garden. A fitness enthusiast, Rowan swims a mile most mornings and is a keen cyclist and occasional horse-rider. He lives in Worcestershire with his partner, who shares his passion for music, the arts and theatre, and he can often be found in the British Library researching all things 1700s.

SURA, 31
LONDON
Pharmacy Dispenser

Sura grew up surrounded by family who offered food as a means to show affection, love and respect. The many Middle Eastern and Asian influences in her heritage – including Turkey, Iraq, Iran, Syria and India – mean she enjoys experimenting with ingredients and flavours from all over the world. Never one to stick to a recipe, Sura loves to improvise in the kitchen and inject her bakes with as much personality as possible. She loves to work with fragrant and floral flavours such as cardamom, rose and orange blossom. She now lives in London with her husband and elderly grandmother. When she's not baking or working, she can be found indulging her passions for travel, architecture and design.

A Baker's Kitchen

You don't need a lot to be able to bake. With an oven, scales, a bowl and a baking sheet you can bake bread, biscuits, scones... add a couple of cake tins and a wooden spoon and you can whip up a cake. So, although the following list seems long, please don't feel overwhelmed – build up your kitchen gradually, as you build up your skills.

BAKING BEANS

An essential to keep the base of a pastry case flat and the sides upright while you blind bake (that is, bake it without its filling). Ceramic baking beans intended for this purpose are handy and reusable, but uncooked dried beans, lentils or rice will work well multiple times, too. Just make sure you store them in a labelled jar afterwards as, once baked, they won't be suitable for eating.

BAKING PAPER AND LINERS

These help prevent sticking. Choose non-stick baking paper (sometimes called parchment). Greaseproof is less sturdy and has a waxy coating that doesn't stand up as well to the heat of the oven. Reusable silicone liners are more expensive, but are easy to use, can be cut to fit your tins and trays (or buy them ready-cut) and can be wiped clean. With proper care they can last for life.

BAKING SHEETS AND TRAYS

A baking sheet is flat with only one raised edge for gripping, making it good for bakes (such as biscuits and pavlovas) that you might want to slide to another surface. A baking tray has a rim or shallow edge all the way around. Aim to have at least one heavy-duty baking sheet, and two or three trays or lightweight sheets.

BAKING TINS

Always use the baking tin that's specified in the recipe as the quantities and baking time have been calculated accordingly. (See the 'You Will Need' lists at the end of each set of ingredients.) A really solid, good-quality tin will withstand repeated baking without scorching or losing its shape. Clean and dry your tins thoroughly after you've used them. Occasionally, a recipe will call a for specialist tin or mould, but in general the following will see you through nicely:

Loaf tins are essential for neat, brick-shaped breads and cakes. They're available in a variety of sizes, but the most-used sizes are 450g (measuring about 19 x 12.5 x 7.5cm) and 900g (measuring about 26 x 12.5 x 7.5cm). Heavy-duty loaf tins won't dent or warp and will give you a better crust than equivalent silicone versions.

Muffin or cupcake tins are what you need for small bakes. They are usually 6- or 12-hole. Non-stick and silicone versions will produce equally good results, so choose what suits you best. Some recipes in the book make 18, so it can be useful to have both 12- and 6-hole versions in your cupboards.

Pudding moulds (mini ones) are a bit of a luxury, but handy for making individual dessert bakes, such as chocolate fondants, or Prue's Sussex Pond Puddings on page 185.

Sandwich (or sponge) tins are essential. Aim to own two 20–20.5cm-diameter sandwich tins, each 4–5cm deep. A third tin is useful for baking American-style layer cakes.

Springform (or springclip) tins are deep metal tins with a spring release. Use them for cakes, tortes, pies, cheesecakes and pull-apart bread rolls because they won't damage the sides of a fragile bake as you remove it.

Swiss roll tins are rectangular (usually 20 x 30cm or 23 x 33cm) and about 2cm deep.

Tart and tartlet tins, available with fluted and straight sides, give the most professional results when made from sturdy metal, such as anodised aluminium. Choose non-stick, loose-bottomed versions for the best results.

Traybake tins are square or rectangular and about 4cm deep, and used for brownies, shortbread, and all traybakes. Buy loose-bottomed tins to help free your bakes easily.

BOWLS

For versatility, sturdiness and durability, heatproof glass and stainless steel bowls are good choices for mixing and whisking, and glass or ceramic are best for melting ingredients over hot water, although plastic bowls are cheaper. (Note, too, that ceramic bowls look pretty but can be heavy.) A very large bowl with a snap-on lid is useful for mixing and rising bread doughs. Incidentally, make your bowls non-slip by resting them on a damp cloth as you mix.

CAKE-DECORATING TURNTABLE

Although not essential, a cake-decorating turntable makes easy work of smoothing out buttercreams or ganache around the sides of a cake. It's especially handy if you're going for a semi-naked effect (such as in the cake on page 123) or perhaps an ombre (see p.267).

COOLING/WIRE RACKS

A large wire rack with legs allows air to circulate around and underneath a bake as it cools, avoiding any sogginess. A wire grill-pan rack makes a good improvisation.

DOUGH SCRAPER

One of the cheapest and most useful pieces of equipment, the dough scraper helps to scoop, scrape and divide bread dough, and makes easy work of cleaning bowls and worktops.

ELECTRIC STAND MIXERS, PROCESSORS AND WHISKS

Lots of the recipes in the book call for a helping hand from an electric gadget, such as a stand mixer. Although these can make life easier, if you're new to baking, don't feel you have to rush out and buy one. Most of the recipes in the book can be made with muscle power – just remember to keep going (with a hand whisk, a wooden spoon, or your bare hands), until you reach the consistency described in the method.

A large-capacity stand mixer is a good investment if you do a lot of baking. Use the whisk attachment for meringues, buttercreams and light sponge mixtures; the paddle or beater attachment for heavier mixtures, such as richer cakes, choux pastry, and savarin-type enriched doughs; and the dough hook for mixing, then kneading bread doughs. A spare bowl will help with multi-element sponges.

An electric hand whisk is a good, versatile choice if you want to make whisked mixtures, creamed sponges, meringues, buttercreams or batter, or mixtures whisked over heat.

A hand-held stick blender (often with a whisk attachment, too) is good for smoothing out fruit sauces and crème pâtissière.

A food processor makes light work of blending fat and flour to make pastry. Use the 'pulse' button to avoid any overworking. It's also good for finely chopping nuts and herbs (a mini version is great for small quantities).

HAND OR BALLOON WHISK
A wire hand whisk can be balloon-shaped or flat; a hand-held rotary whisk consists of a pair of beaters in a metal frame. Any of these is essential, even if you have an electric version.

KNIVES
The better the knife, the better your knife skills. Stainless steel knives are easy to keep clean, but need to be sharpened regularly; carbon-steel knives are more expensive, but easier to keep sharp. Gather a medium knife, about 20cm long; a small knife (useful for pastry work, trimming edges, and making decorations); and a good-quality serrated bread knife (for sawing through crusts).

LAME
A lame is useful for scoring bread – it's like a double-sided razor blade on a handle.

MEASURING EQUIPMENT
Baking is a science and, for perfect results, precision is essential.

Digital scales are particularly useful. As well as weighing tiny ingredients and switching easily between units, you can 'zero' ingredients you've already weighed, then add further ingredients to the same bowl, weighing each as you go.

Measuring jugs, even if you have digital scales, are a must. Pick a heat-resistant and microwave-safe jug that starts at 50ml (ideally) or 100ml, and goes up to 2 litres.

Measuring spoons do a far better job than everyday spoons (teaspoons, dessert spoons, tablespoons), which will give inconsistent results. Spoon measures in this book are level, not heaped or rounded, unless specified.

METAL SPOON
A large, long metal spoon is invaluable for folding wet ingredients into dry.

OVEN THERMOMETER
Built-in oven thermostats can be inconsistent and will become less efficient with age, so an oven thermometer is a way to make sure your oven reaches the right temperature before you bake, as well as to identify the hot and cool spots to avoid uneven bakes. If you don't have a thermometer, know your oven – increase or decrease the temperature or baking time to get the right results, as needed.

PALETTE KNIFE
An offset palette knife (with a kink near the handle) is useful for spreading icings and delicate mixtures where you need a smooth, precise result. A straight palette knife is good for lifting and moving bakes from one surface to another.

PASTRY BRUSH
Opt for a heat- and dishwasher-proof, medium pastry brush. It's a must-have you'll use not only for glazing pastry and bread, but for tasks

such as brushing down sugar crystals from the sides of a pan as you make caramel.

PASTRY CUTTERS

Pick a double-sided (plain on one side, fluted on the other) nest of metal cutters. A pizza wheel-cutter is handy for cutting straight lines (such as for the lattice strips in the Pandowdy Swamp Pie on page 171 or the layered dough in Paul's Rainbow-coloured Bagels on page 81). Shaped cutters are infinite and lovely, too.

PIPING BAGS AND NOZZLES

The recipes in this book use both reusable and paper piping bags in various sizes. Piping nozzles, made from metal or plastic, range from wide, round tips for piping choux pastry and meringue, to star-shaped for icings, to fine writing tips for delicate work. Set the nozzle in the bag, stand it in a jug or mug for support, then fill. Twist the top before you pipe.

PROVING BAGS

Although not strictly necessary (covering with oiled cling film will do), proving bags (ideally two) are reusable, which makes them kinder to the environment. Slide your dough inside on a baking tray and inflate the bag a little to stop the dough sticking to it as it rises.

ROLLING PIN

A fairly heavy wooden pin about 6–7cm in diameter and without handles will make the easiest work of rolling out pastry.

RUBBER SPATULA

A strong and flexible spatula is useful for mixing, folding and scraping with ease.

SIEVE

Every baker needs a sieve – to combine flour with raising agents; remove lumps from icing and sugars; and for straining and puréeing. Go for a large metal sieve that will sit over your largest mixing bowl for sifting tasks, and a smaller, tea-strainer-sized one for dusting.

SUGAR THERMOMETER/ COOKING THERMOMETER

Essential for sugar work (and deep-frying), a sugar thermometer will ensure your sugar reaches the correct temperature if, for example, you're making caramel or nougat, or tempering chocolate – among other baking tasks. Pick one that's easy to read and can clip on to the side of the pan. A thermometer with a probe will help you to measure the internal temperatures of your bakes for doneness, too.

TIMER

A digital kitchen timer with seconds as well as minutes (and a loud bell) is essential – don't rely on just your oven timer. Set for a minute or two less than the suggested time in your recipe (especially if you are uncertain of your oven) – you can always increase the oven time.

WOODEN SPOON

Cheap, heat-resistant, and safe on non-stick pans, a wooden spoon mixes, beats, creams and stirs – the essentials of good baking. (You can even use the handle to shape brandy snaps and tuiles.) Store your savoury and sweet spoons separately, as wood can absorb strong flavours.

ZESTER

A long-handled zester is the best and quickest way to remove the zest from citrus fruits (use unwaxed citrus fruits for zesting). Pick one that's sturdy and easy to hold.

A Baker's Larder

Most of the bakes throughout this book use ingredients that you'll find in supermarkets. Keep the following in your store cupboard and, whether you need to whip up something for a cake sale, find an activity for the kids for the afternoon, or create a dinner-party showstopper, you'll be ready to start baking. As a rule of thumb: the best-quality ingredients tend to give the best results.

BAKING POWDER, BICARBONATE OF SODA AND CREAM OF TARTAR

Chemical raising agents, all these ingredients increase the lightness and volume of cakes and small bakes, and some types of biscuit and pastry. Always use the amount given in the recipe – but check the date stamps before you start, as raising agents will lose their potency over time. If you've run out of baking powder, you can easily make your own: for 1 teaspoon of baking powder combine ½ teaspoon of cream of tartar with ¼ teaspoon of bicarbonate of soda. If you are making a gluten-free bake, bear in mind that baking powder should be gluten-free, but some manufacturers add filling agents that may contain gluten. Always check the labels.

BUTTER AND OTHER FATS

Most of the recipes in this book use unsalted butter, as it has a delicate flavour, adds a good, even colour (perhaps because it contains less whey than salted), and allows you to season your bake to taste yourself, as relevant. Store butter tightly wrapped in the fridge, well away from strong flavours. When relevant, a recipe will tell you whether to use butter chilled (from the fridge) or softened at room temperature (in that case, don't be tempted to soften in the microwave – you're looking for a texture that yields easily when pressed with a finger, but holds the shape, not melted). Cubed butter enables you to add small amounts at a time and makes the butter easier to combine with the other ingredients.

Lard, from pigs, gives a short, flaky texture to traditional hot-water-crust pastry so that it bakes to a crisp, golden finish. White solid vegetable fat is a good alternative.

Dairy-free spreads, made from vegetable and sunflower oils, make good substitutes in most recipes that require softened or room-temperature butter, but always check the label to make sure it's good for baking beforehand. Some are made specifically for baking and you can use them straight from the fridge. They give good results, but may lack that buttery flavour. Avoid spreads designed for use on bread/crackers – they contain too much water and not enough fat to make good baking ingredients.

Solid coconut oil is a good option for dairy-free and vegan recipes, but isn't a like-for-like butter substitute.

Suet, from cows in its non-vegetarian form, gives a light, soft pastry rather than a very crisp or flaky one. Suet is more solid than butter or lard and melts much more slowly, forming tiny pockets in the dough as it cooks. Most supermarkets now sell vegetarian suet, too (you'll need it for Prue's Sussex Pond Puddings on page 185).

Oil often pops up in bakes these days. Vegetable oil is a good all-rounder, but in baking, sunflower oil gives the best results as it's especially light and mildly flavoured.

CHOCOLATE

Chocolate is a must in baking – from shards and shavings to ganache and buttercream, it features in many of the recipes in this book.

Dark chocolate, with around 70% cocoa solids, is the kind most used in these recipes as it gives a good balance of flavour – chocolate with a higher percentage (75% and above) may be too bitter and dry for general baking. Some baking recipes will recommend 54% dark, which is a little sweeter.

Milk chocolate has a much milder and sweeter flavour – choose a good-quality favourite, and expect the best results from milk chocolate with good amounts of cocoa solids.

White chocolate doesn't contain any cocoa solids, just cocoa butter. Look out for brands with 30% or more cocoa butter as a measure of quality. White chocolate sets less firmly than dark or milk chocolate owing to the higher fat content, and melts at a lower temperature, so take care as it easily scorches and becomes unusable.

COCOA POWDER

A dark, unsweetened powder made from pure cocoa beans after they have been dried and had all the cocoa butter removed. Cocoa powder is very bitter, strongly flavoured and gives a powerful hit. Never substitute cocoa powder with drinking chocolate, which contains milk powder and sugar, as well as cocoa powder itself.

CREAM

For best results, chill cream thoroughly before whipping (in really hot weather chill the bowl and whisk before you start, too).

Buttermilk, sometimes labelled 'cultured buttermilk', is low-fat or non-fat milk plus a bacterial culture to give it an acidic tang. It is often used along with bicarbonate of soda to add lightness as well as flavour to scones and cakes.

Crème fraîche is a soured cream with a creamy, tangy flavour. It won't whip, but you can use it for fillings, toppings and serving.

Double cream contains at least 48% butterfat. It whips well and has a richer flavour than whipping cream. The extra-rich type of double cream available is designed for spooning, rather than for whipping or for making ganache.

Lactose-free and soya-based dairy-free creams can give varied results, and are usually unsuitable for whipping.

Single cream contains 18% butterfat and is good for adding to sauces and fillings, for adding richness to rubbed-in mixtures, or for pouring over desserts and pastries.

Soured cream has only 18% butterfat. It is made by introducing a bacterial culture to cream, giving a naturally sour tang.

Whipping cream usually contains at least 36% butterfat and is designed to whip well without being overly rich.

DRIED FRUIT

Keep stores of dried fruit out of direct sunlight and tightly sealed in containers. Vine fruit, such as raisins, sultanas and currants, have a long shelf-life, but will always be best bought when you need them. Soft-dried apricots, as well as dried figs, cranberries, blueberries, sour cherries, and dates, can replace vine fruits in many recipes. They add sweetness and moisture to cakes and breads, which is useful if you want to reduce refined sugar.

EGGS

When it comes to eggs, size really does matter. Unless otherwise stated, all the recipes in this book use medium eggs. If the eggs are too small, a sponge may not rise properly and look thin or dry; too big and a pastry or bread dough may be too wet or soft to handle.

For baking, use eggs at room temperature, so take them out of the fridge 30–60 minutes before you start cooking. If you forget, pop them into a bowl of lukewarm water for a couple of minutes.

Spare egg whites will keep for 3–4 days in a sealed container or jar in the fridge, or for up to a month in the freezer (defrost overnight in the fridge before using; yolks can't be frozen).

EXTRACTS AND FLAVOURINGS

Avoid synthetic flavourings as much as you can – they often have an aftertaste that will spoil your hard work. Here's a guide to the best to use.

Almond extract may be pricey, but most recipes need only a few drops. Avoid anything marked 'flavouring'.

Ground spices are best when you use them fresh, but if you're storing them, do so in screw-topped jars, rather than open packets, to prolong their flavour.

Vanilla is usually the most expensive flavouring used in baking, although you need to use only small amounts of the real thing. Vanilla extract – labelled 'pure' or 'natural' – costs more than vanilla essence, which might contain artificial flavourings. Vanilla paste is made from the seeds of the pods and has a thicker texture and more concentrated flavour. Best of all, though, are vanilla pods, which you can split to scrape out the tiny seeds to flavour custards, crème pâtissière and fillings. Don't throw away the pods: rinse and dry carefully, then put them in a jar of caster sugar to make vanilla sugar.

FLOUR

Whether made from wheat or other grains, flour has to be the most valued ingredient in the baker's larder. Avoid poor-quality, out-of-date or stale flour, as this will affect the result and taste of the final bake. Always buy the best and freshest flour you can afford.

Cornflour is a finely milled white powder added to biscuits to give a delicate crumb, and used to thicken custard and crème pâtissière.

Gluten-free flours are wheat-free mixtures of several ingredients, including rice, potato, tapioca, maize, chickpea, broad bean, white sorghum or buckwheat – depending on the brand. Ready-mixed gluten-free flours sometimes suggest adding xanthan gum (a powder sold in small tubs) to improve the texture and crumb of your bake – check the packet and, if your flour mixture doesn't already include it, add 1 teaspoon of xanthan gum per 150g gluten-free flour. Some gluten-free flours need a little more liquid than wheat flour doughs, so you can't substitute them exactly, but it is well worth experimenting.

Plain flour is a type of wheat flour used for making pastry, pancakes and rich fruit cakes, for example, and has no added raising agents.

Rye flour has a deep, dark flavour that works well in breads, particularly sourdoughs. It's low in gluten, which makes it harder to knead than wheat flours, and the dough rises less well. Available as wholegrain and a finer 'light' rye, which has had some of the bran sifted out, it is useful for crackers and adding to wheat flour for savoury pastry recipes.

Self-raising flour has added baking powder and is most often used in sponge-cake recipes to give a light, risen texture. If you run out of self-raising flour you can easily make your own: add 4 teaspoons of baking powder to every 225g plain flour, sifting them together a couple of times. Sponge self-raising flour is more expensive than regular self-raising, but is slightly 'softer' and silkier, as it is more finely milled.

Semolina flour is a slightly gritty, pale yellow flour made from durum wheat, and often used for pasta and Italian-style breads (as well as semolina pudding).

Speciality wheat flours are created from wheat varieties that are specifically grown to make flour for baking ciabatta, pizza bases, and baguettes.

Spelt flour comes from the same family as wheat, but has a slightly different genetic make-up and a richer and more nutty flavour – it is good for most recipes that call for flour, except very delicate biscuits and sponges.

Stoneground flour means that the grain (wheat, rye, spelt and so on) is milled between large stones instead of steel rollers, giving a coarser texture and fuller flavour.

Strong bread flour is made from wheat with a higher ratio of protein to starch than the cake and pastry flours. This increased ratio is crucial to bread-making: as you knead the dough, the protein develops into strands of gluten that stretch as the gases produced by the yeast expand, enabling the dough to rise. Strong bread flour has about 12–16% protein, which is ideal for most breads. Extra-strong or Canadian strong flour has even more (15–17%) – good for bagels or larger loaves.

Wholemeal or wholegrain flours are made from the complete wheat kernel, making them far more nutritious than white flours (which are made using 75% of the cleaned wheat kernel, and have most of the wheat bran and wheatgerm removed). The small specks of bran in these flours mean that they give a dough that rises less well than one made with all white flour. Wholemeal plain flour has been milled to make it lighter and more suitable for making pastry and cakes.

NUTS

Buy nuts in small quantities to use up quickly (always before the use-by date) – the high oil content means that once opened, nuts can quickly turn rancid. If you're storing them, do so in an airtight container in a cool, dark place. Most nuts benefit from being lightly toasted before use, to impart a richer, nuttier flavour to the finished bake.

Almonds are incredibly versatile – ground, chopped, flaked (toasted and untoasted) and whole (blanched or unblanched). To blanch (remove the skins) yourself, put the nuts in a small pan, add water to cover and bring to the boil. Remove the pan from the heat and drain, then slip the nuts out of their casings. Dry on kitchen paper.

Hazelnuts are usually ready-blanched (without their brown papery skins) or ground.

Pistachios are easy to find shelled and unsalted, but they usually come with their papery skins attached. To reveal the deep-green colour of the nuts, carefully tip them into a pan of boiling water. Remove from the heat, leave for 1 minute, then drain. Transfer the nuts to a clean, dry tea towel and rub gently to loosen the skins, then peel if necessary. Ready-ground pistachios are also available these days.

Walnuts and **pecans**, usually halved or chopped, are interchangeable in most baking recipes as they share a similar texture and appearance (walnuts are slightly more bitter). Gently toasting walnuts and pecans in a medium-heat oven gives them a much deeper, richer flavour.

SUGAR

Different sugars combine and interact with other ingredients in different ways, affecting the end results of the bake. Always use the sugar the recipe specifies. Sugar doesn't have a shelf life and will keep indefinitely in an airtight container in a cool, dark place.

Caster sugar comes as both refined white and unrefined golden. White provides sweetness with a neutral colour and flavour that is, for example, perfect for white meringues or very pale sponges. Unrefined golden caster sugar has a slight caramel, rich flavour. Use it when having a warmer colour in your final bake is not an issue. The fine grains of caster sugar break down easily during beating or creaming with butter for sponges, melt quickly for lemon curd, and disappear in pastry mixtures.

Fondant icing sugar sets hard, so it's good for decorating as it doesn't smudge. It contains glucose syrup to give a smooth, glossy finish.

Granulated sugar, available as white or golden, has bigger grains that take longer to dissolve. Keep it for making sugar syrups and drizzles, and for sprinkling on top of bakes to give a satisfying crunch.

Icing sugar is also available as refined (white) and unrefined (golden). Again, the unrefined version has a pale caramel colour and flavour. Use white icing sugar for icings, fillings and frostings that need to be very pale or that are to be coloured with food colouring. Sift icing sugar before use to remove any lumps so that your icing is perfectly smooth.

Jam sugar contains added pectin to help jam set, making it good for making jams that use fruits without high natural levels of pectin – raspberries, strawberries, apricots and ripe cherries, among them.

Muscovado sugars come as light muscovado and dark muscovado. These add a stronger, warmer caramel or molasses flavour and darker colour to bakes, but they can make them more moist and heavy. They are good in rich fruity cakes, gingerbreads, parkins, and spice cakes. Press out any lumps with the back of a spoon before using.

SYRUP AND TREACLE

Golden syrup and thick black treacle add a rich, toffee-ish flavour, as well as sweetness, to bakes. They can be difficult to measure if you're spooning out of a tin, so warm the measuring spoon in a mug of just-boiled water before scooping, or stand the syrup or treacle tin in a bowl of boiled water for a few minutes to loosen the stickiness. Easier is to use a squeezy bottle – many brands of golden syrup now come readily available this way (similarly, for honey). Maple syrup has a lighter texture than golden syrup, but a distinctive flavour that works particularly well with nuts, and, of course, over pancakes.

YEAST

Yeast is a living organism that makes bread doughs rise. It needs moisture, gentle warmth and flour (or sugar) to stimulate its growth and the production of carbon dioxide, which expands the dough. The recipes in this book use fast-action dried yeast, available in 7g sachets or in tubs as easy blend or instant dried yeast. Always weigh your yeast, unless it's coming from a sachet, and add the yeast powder to the flour, never to the liquid. If you add it with the salt, do so on opposite sides of the bowl, as salt (and too much sugar) retards its growth. (And hot water kills it.) If you use too much yeast in a bake, the dough will be lively, but the baked loaf may have a strong aftertaste and will go stale more quickly. If you use too little, the dough will take longer to rise and prove, but it will have a deeper flavour and will most likely keep better.

CHAPTER ONE

Random Acts
of Kindness

Recipes

3 tbsp whole milk
1 tea bag (breakfast
   or strong black tea)
50g 70% dark chocolate,
   roughly chopped
125g unsalted butter,
   softened
150g light muscovado sugar
75g golden caster sugar
2 eggs, lightly beaten
175g plain flour
75g white rye flour
1 tsp baking powder
1 tsp ground ginger
1 tsp ground cinnamon
½ tsp ground cardamom
¼ tsp ground cloves
¼ tsp freshly ground
   black pepper
pinch of salt
4 tbsp granulated sugar
4 tbsp icing sugar, sifted

YOU WILL NEED
2 baking sheets,
   greased, then lined
   with baking paper

Makes about 30

Hands on 20 mins

plus chilling

Bake 15 mins

Chai Crackle Cookies

Tea and sympathy in cookie form. These cookies have all the spices of Indian chai, coupled with chocolate for good measure. Chill the dough for at least 4 hours but, if you have time, overnight is best.

1. Heat the milk either in a microwave or small pan to just below boiling. Add the tea bag, stir well and leave to brew for 5 minutes. Squeeze the tea bag into the milk to extract the flavour and remove.

2. Meanwhile, melt the chocolate either in a microwave on a low setting or in a heatproof bowl set over a pan of barely simmering water. Stir until smooth, then remove from the heat.

3. Beat the butter and muscovado and caster sugars in a stand mixer fitted with the beater, on medium speed for 3–5 minutes, until pale and creamy, scraping down the sides of the bowl from time to time. Add the beaten eggs, half at a time, beating between each addition.

4. Sift both flours, the baking powder, spices, pepper and salt into the bowl and mix until just combined. Add the tea-infused milk and melted chocolate, then beat for 1 minute, or until combined. Cover and chill the dough for at least 4 hours, or preferably overnight.

5. Heat the oven to 180°C/160°C fan/Gas 4.

6. Tip the granulated sugar into one bowl and the icing sugar into another. Using your hands, shape the cookie dough into neat, walnut-sized balls (you should get about 30 balls altogether).

7. Working in batches, tip the balls into the granulated sugar, rolling to coat. Remove, shaking off any excess and transfer to the icing sugar, rolling again to thickly coat. Space the cookies well apart on the lined baking sheets to allow them to spread during baking.

8. Bake the cookies for 13–15 minutes, until slightly puffed and starting to firm up around the edges. Leave to cool on the baking sheets for 2–3 minutes, then transfer to a wire rack to cool completely.

FOR THE FILLING
65g blanched hazelnuts
100g unsalted butter
150g caster sugar
80g 70% dark chocolate, chopped
40g cocoa powder

FOR THE DOUGH
275g plain flour
5g fast-action dried yeast
25g caster sugar
½ tsp fine salt
2 eggs, beaten
50ml whole milk
80g unsalted butter, cubed and softened

FOR THE SYRUP
100g caster sugar

YOU WILL NEED
900g loaf tin, greased, then lined (base, sides and overhanging the short ends) with baking paper
proving bag (optional)

Makes 1 loaf

Hands on 30 mins

plus proving

Bake 45 mins

JUDGE'S RECIPE

Paul's Chocolate Babka

Best on the day, this fudgy chocolate babka is easy to wrap and take with you to share with a friend alongside a good cup of coffee.

1. Heat the oven to 200°C/180°C fan/Gas 6.

2. Make the filling. Tip the hazelnuts into a baking tray and roast in the bottom of the oven for 4–5 minutes, tossing occasionally, until light golden. Tip onto a chopping board, leave to cool, then roughly chop half the hazelnuts and finely chop the remainder. Set aside.

3. Place the butter, sugar and chocolate in a pan and melt very slowly over a low heat, stirring until smooth and combined. Remove from the heat and stir in the cocoa powder. Pour into a bowl and leave to cool and thicken slightly.

4. Meanwhile, make the dough. Tip the flour into the bowl of a stand mixer fitted with the dough hook, add the yeast to one side of the bowl and the sugar and salt to the other side.

5. Make a well in the centre and pour in the eggs and milk, then mix on slow speed for 2–3 minutes, until firm.

6. Increase the speed to medium and add the butter, a little at a time. Mix well between each addition, allowing the butter to incorporate before adding more.

7. Once you have added all the butter, continue kneading with the dough hook on medium speed through the sticky stage, until you have a ball of smooth, silky, shiny dough.

8. Lightly flour a work surface and roll out the dough to a 40 x 30cm rectangle, with a long edge closest to you.

9. Spread the cooled chocolate mixture over the dough, leaving a 1cm border all around. Sprinkle all the toasted hazelnuts over the top.

Continues overleaf

10. Starting from the long edge closest to you, roll up the dough into a tight spiral, with the seam underneath.

11. Trim about 2cm off each end to neaten, then turn the roll through 90° clockwise so that a short end is closest to you. Using a large, sharp knife or a pizza cutter, slice lengthways, down through the middle of the dough, cutting it into 2 long pieces.

12. With the cut-sides facing upwards, gently press the top end of each half together to seal, then lift the right half over the left half, followed by the left half over the right half. Repeat, twisting the dough to make a two-stranded plait, then gently press the bottom ends together to seal.

13. Carefully lift the loaf into the lined tin and cover with a clean tea towel (or place in a proving bag, if you have one). Leave at room temperature for about 2 hours (or in a proving drawer for 1 hour), until doubled in size.

14. Fifteen minutes before the end of the proving time, heat the oven to 190°C/170°C fan/Gas 5.

15. When the babka has proved, bake it for 15 minutes, then reduce the oven temperature to 170°C/150°C fan/Gas 3 and cook for a further 25–30 minutes, until a skewer inserted into the centre comes out clean.

16. While the babka is baking, make the syrup. Tip the sugar and 100ml water into a small pan, bring to the boil over a medium heat, stirring until the sugar dissolves. Reduce the heat and simmer, without stirring, for 5 minutes, until syrupy. Leave to cool.

17. When the babka is ready, transfer it in the tin to a wire rack. Brush the cooled syrup over the hot babka, then leave in the tin until warm enough to handle. Turn out onto the wire rack and serve warm or at room temperature.

FOR THE CAKE

150g salted butter, softened,
plus extra for greasing
150g caster sugar
3 eggs, beaten
100g self-raising flour
25g ground almonds
1 tbsp lemon juice
finely grated zest of
½ unwaxed lemon
25g pistachio flour or finely
ground Iranian pistachios
5–6 drops pistachio extract
green food-colouring paste
(optional)
4 tbsp apricot or seedless
raspberry jam

FOR THE MARZIPAN

160g ground almonds
80g icing sugar
80g caster sugar
4 tsp pasteurised egg white
1 drop almond extract

YOU WILL NEED

15cm square cake tin,
greased
17 x 30cm strip of 2-in-1
parchment and foil
ruler
8 pieces of pistachio-
coloured paper, each
measuring 20 x 3cm
8 lengths of narrow ribbon
(gold is pretty), each
30cm long (2.5m of
ribbon altogether)

Mini Lemon and Pistachio Battenbergs

We've given this traditional cake a modern twist, not only by making mini versions, but also by making them in a delicious combination of lemon and pistachio flavours, all wrapped in homemade almond paste and tied with a ribbon.

1. Heat the oven to 180°C/160°C fan/Gas 4. Fold the strip of parchment in half and, holding the folded edge, fold it over by 7cm, then open up the foil on either side and re-crease the centre folds to make a divider. Place the divider in the centre of the tin.

2. Place the butter and sugar in the bowl of a stand mixer fitted with the beater and beat for 5 minutes until light and fluffy. Gradually add the eggs, until combined, adding 1 tablespoon of the flour to prevent the mixture curdling, if necessary. Fold the remaining flour into the mixture.

3. Halve the mixture and add the ground almonds and lemon juice and zest to one half, and the pistachio flour and pistachio extract to the other half. Add a drop of green food colouring to the pistachio mixture, if using.

4. Transfer the mixtures into the tin – the lemon in one half and the pistachio in the other. Bake for 25–30 minutes until golden brown and risen. Leave to cool in the tin for 5 minutes, then turn out onto a wire rack to cool completely.

5. Separate the cakes into yellow and green and trim the tops and sides to level and neaten. Cut each cake in half horizontally – to make 2 yellow and 2 green 15 x 7.5cm (or thereabouts) rectangles. Spread the top of each cake with some of the jam.

Continues overleaf

6. Make two sandwiches, each with 1 green cake and 1 yellow. Cut each sandwich into 4 even strips – to make eight 15 x 1.5cm (approximately) finger sandwiches. Turn the strips over to lay flat and spread with a little more of the jam.

7. Stack the strips back together in alternate stacks to make 4 long, thin Battenbergs. Trim the ends and set aside.

8. To make the marzipan, place the ground almonds, icing sugar and caster sugar in a small bowl. Add the egg white and the almond extract and mix with your hands until it comes together to make a smooth paste.

9. Divide the marzipan into 4 equal portions. Roll out the first portion on a work surface lightly dusted with icing sugar, taking care it doesn't stick to the work surface, into a neat square (roughly 15cm) and spread with more jam. Trim one end using a ruler to give you a straight edge and lay the long side of a Battenberg stack against this neat edge. Roll up the stack in the marzipan, trim the excess, and cut in half to give you 2 mini Battenbergs. Repeat with the remaining 3 portions of marzipan to make 8 mini Battenbergs altogether.

10. Wrap 1 piece of pistachio-coloured paper neatly around the middle of each mini Battenberg. Tie a length of ribbon around each cake to secure the paper and finish off.

FOR THE DOUGH

500g strong white
   bread flour
40g unsalted butter,
   softened
40g caster sugar
2 x 7g sachets fast-action
   dried yeast
½ tsp salt
325ml whole milk,
   plus extra for glazing
1–2 tbsp icing sugar,
   for dusting

FOR THE FILLING

400ml double cream
1 tsp vanilla extract
12 tbsp homemade or
   good-quality raspberry
   or strawberry jam

YOU WILL NEED

2 baking sheets,
   greased, then lined
   with baking paper
large piping bag fitted with
   a large closed star nozzle

Makes
12

Hands on
30 mins

plus rising

Bake
15 mins

Devonshire Splits

Who wouldn't welcome fluffy sweet buns, filled with cream and jam as an afternoon tea treat with a friend or family member? They make a lovely, all-in-one alternative to a Devonshire scone.

1. Tip the flour into the bowl of a stand mixer fitted with the dough hook. Add the butter, sugar, yeast and salt and mix to combine.

2. Gently warm the milk either in a microwave or small pan over a low heat. Add to the bowl with the flour mixture and mix for 5 minutes, or until the dough is smooth and elastic.

3. Turn out the dough onto the work surface and shape it into a neat ball. Place in an oiled bowl, cover and leave to rise for about 1 hour, until doubled in size.

4. Turn out the dough onto the work surface again, and knead for 30 seconds to knock out any large air pockets.

5. Weigh the dough and divide it into 12 equal pieces. Shape each piece into a neat ball with the seam on the underside and arrange on the lined baking sheets, leaving plenty of space in between each one to allow for spreading during proving and baking. Cover loosely and prove for about 45 minutes, until almost doubled in size.

6. Meanwhile, heat the oven to 190°C/170°C fan/Gas 5.

7. Lightly brush the top of each bun with milk. Bake for about 15 minutes, or until well risen and golden brown and the buns sound hollow when tapped on the underside. Transfer to a wire rack to cool to room temperature.

8. Whip the cream and vanilla to soft peaks, then spoon into the piping bag.

9. Using a serrated knife, cut a deep slit into the top of each bun. Spread the jam on one side of the split and pipe a generous swirl of whipped cream alongside. Dust with icing sugar to finish.

Serves
12

Hands on
1½ hours

Bake
25 mins

plus chilling

BAKER'S FAVOURITE

Marc's Chocolate Brownie Drip Cake

My daughters, Jasmine and Rosie, love this cake. They buzz with excitement whenever they know I'm baking it and I love making it for them throughout the year (but it's always a high point for their birthdays, especially). I have to be quick to get my slice – and there's no better accompaniment to a mug of hot tea.

FOR THE SPONGE
50g cocoa powder
2 tsp instant coffee
6 tbsp just-boiled water
100g unsalted butter, softened
275g caster sugar
3 large eggs
175g self-raising flour, sifted
1 tsp baking powder, sifted
100g 70% dark chocolate chips

FOR THE CHOCOLATE GANACHE
200g 70% dark chocolate, chopped
200ml double cream

FOR THE CHANTILLY CREAM
200ml double cream
1 tbsp icing sugar
1 tsp vanilla extract

FOR THE CHOCOLATE DRIPS
75g milk chocolate
75ml double cream

TO DECORATE
100g each milk, white and dark chocolate, at room temperature

YOU WILL NEED
15cm sandwich tins x 3, greased, then base-lined with baking paper
medium piping bag fitted with a medium plain nozzle
20cm cake board (optional)
cake scraper
cake-decorating comb (optional)
squeezy bottle or small, paper piping bag (optional)

1. Heat the oven to 180°C/160°C fan/Gas 4.

2. Make the sponge. Mix the cocoa and coffee with the just-boiled water to a smooth paste, then set aside.

3. Beat the butter and sugar in a stand mixer fitted with the beater, on medium speed for 3–5 minutes, until pale and creamy, scraping down the sides of the bowl from time to time.

4. Add the eggs, one at time, beating well between each addition and adding a little of your flour if the mixture begins to curdle. Beat in the cooled cocoa/coffee paste, then fold in the flour, baking powder and chocolate chips until fully combined.

5. Divide the mixture equally between the lined tins and level with a palette knife. Bake for 20–25 minutes, until slightly coming away from the edges and a skewer inserted into the centre of each sponge comes out clean. Leave to cool in the tins for 5 minutes, then turn out onto a wire rack and leave to cool completely.

6. Meanwhile, make the chocolate ganache. Place the chocolate in a medium heatproof bowl. Pour the cream into a small pan and bring just to the boil over a medium heat, then pour it over the chocolate. Leave for 5 minutes, then stir until smooth and glossy. Leave to cool, then beat with an electric hand whisk until light and fluffy.

Continues overleaf

7. Make the Chantilly cream. Using an electric hand whisk, whisk the cream, icing sugar and vanilla together to soft peaks. Spoon into the piping bag fitted with a medium plain nozzle and twist the end to seal.

8. To assemble, spread a blob of ganache on the cake board or serving plate and place one sponge on top. Pipe half the Chantilly on top, add the second sponge and repeat with the remaining Chantilly. Top with the last sponge.

9. Using a palette knife, spread the sides and top of the cake with the chocolate ganache, then using a scraper, scrape the top and sides until smooth. If you wish, you can use a decorating comb to gently comb grooves into the chocolate ganache. Chill the cake for 30 minutes.

10. Make the chocolate drips. Place the chocolate in a small heatproof bowl. Pour the cream into a small pan and bring just to the boil over a medium heat, then pour it over the chocolate. Leave for 5 minutes, then stir until smooth. Leave to cool a little until thickened slightly.

11. Place the chocolate mixture in a squeezy bottle, or in a small piping bag (twist to seal and snip the end). Pipe drips down the edge of the cake (it's fine if the drips make puddles at the bottom), then spread the remainder on top. (You can use a teaspoon to create the drips, if you prefer.) Chill for 30 minutes, until the chocolate has set.

12. Using a potato peeler, shave curls of white, milk and dark chocolate onto the top of the cake to decorate.

300g gluten-free plain flour
175g unsalted butter,
    cubed and chilled
1 tbsp poppy seeds
5 tbsp ice-cold water
2 tsp white wine vinegar
    or cider vinegar

FOR THE FILLING
500g peeled and
    deseeded squash
    (preferably butternut
    or queen), peeled weight,
    cut into chunks
2 onions, cut into
    thick slices
2 tbsp olive oil
2 roasted red peppers
    from a jar, drained
150g kale or cavolo
    nero, trimmed
5 eggs
2 egg yolks
350ml double cream
1 egg white
150g hard goat's cheese
    or feta, crumbled
1 tbsp hazelnuts
1 tbsp pumpkin seeds
small handful of flat-leaf
    parsley leaves
a few dill sprigs
1 tbsp extra-virgin olive
    oil or rapeseed oil
1 tsp cider vinegar
½–1 tsp za'atar (optional)
salt and freshly ground
    black pepper

YOU WILL NEED
20 x 30cm baking or
    tart tin (4cm deep)
baking beans or rice

Roasted Butternut Squash and Goat's Cheese Tart

This vegetable-laden, gluten-free tart makes a very welcome lunch or light supper for a time-poor friend who would be grateful for something tasty and nourishing ready to go. It's brilliantly adaptable – swap the vegetables for roasted asparagus tips, chargrilled courgette slices or even peas. And feel free to change the cheese, too – any cheese that's sharp and tangy will work.

Serves
6

Hands on
1 hour
plus chilling

Bake
50 mins

1. Make the pastry. Tip the flour into a large mixing bowl and season well with salt and pepper. Using a round-bladed knife, cut the butter into the flour until the pieces are half their original size. Using your fingertips, rub the butter into the flour until the mixture resembles fine breadcrumbs. Stir in the poppy seeds.

2. Add the ice-cold water and the vinegar and mix again with the knife to bring the mixture together. Using your hands, press and gently knead the mixture into a smooth ball, then flatten into a rectangle. Cover and chill for about 2 hours, until firm.

3. Roll out the pastry on a lightly floured work surface until it's large enough to line the base and sides of the baking or tart tin (it should be about 3mm thick).

4. Line the tin with the pastry, pressing it neatly into the corners and grooves. Trim the excess, prick the base with a fork and refrigerate for 30 minutes.

5. Heat the oven to 180°C/160°C fan/Gas 4.

6. Make the filling. Tip the squash and onions into a roasting tin. Season well with salt and pepper and toss in the olive oil. Roast in the top half the oven for 30 minutes, until the vegetables are tender and starting to turn golden brown at the edges.

Continues overleaf

7. While the vegetables are roasting, blind bake the pastry case. Line the pastry with scrunched-up baking paper, then fill with baking beans or rice. Bake for about 20 minutes, until starting to turn crisp and golden at the edges. Remove the paper and beans or rice and return to the oven for another 5 minutes to cook the base.

8. Meanwhile, dry the roasted peppers on kitchen paper and cut into large, bite-sized pieces. Tear the kale or cavolo nero into large pieces, discarding any tough stalks, and lightly steam until just wilted, then pat dry on kitchen paper.

9. In a jug, whisk together the whole eggs, egg yolks and double cream, then season well with salt and pepper.

10. Lightly beat the egg white and brush it over the inside of the pastry case to coat evenly – this will seal any holes or cracks and stop the filling making the pastry soggy. Return to the oven for 1 minute.

11. Arrange the roasted squash, onions, roasted pepper and kale or cavolo nero evenly over the pastry case and pour in the egg and cream mixture. Sprinkle the crumbled goat's cheese or feta over the top. Bake the tart on the middle shelf for about 20 minutes, until the filling is set and the top golden.

12. While the tart is baking, toast the hazelnuts and pumpkin seeds on a baking tray on the lowest shelf in the oven for 3–4 minutes, until starting to colour. Leave to cool slightly, then roughly chop.

13. In a bowl, mix the herbs with the extra-virgin olive oil and the vinegar, and season with salt and pepper. Scatter the herb mixture and the toasted nuts and seeds over the tart, then sprinkle with za'atar (if using). Serve cut into squares or wedges.

50g unsalted butter
50g caster sugar
50g golden syrup
50g plain flour
50g flaked almonds
50g candied orange peel,
    chopped into 5mm dice
50g crystallised ginger,
    chopped into 5mm dice
150g orange-flavoured
    milk chocolate, broken
    into pieces

YOU WILL NEED
3 baking trays, lined
    with baking paper
5–6cm round cutter
    (optional)

Makes
24

Hands on
25 mins

Bake
10 mins

Mini Orange and Ginger Florentines

These dainty biscuits are delicious with coffee or as petits fours after dinner – parcel them up prettily and offer them as a thank-you-for-having-me. We've used crystallised ginger and orange, but flaked coconut, raisins, glacé cherries, dried cranberries, or chopped hazelnuts or apricots are delicious, too.

1. Heat the oven to 180°C/160°C fan/Gas 4.

2. Place the butter, sugar and syrup in a small pan and cook over a medium heat for 2–3 minutes, stirring until the sugar dissolves.

3. Remove from the heat and add the flour, almonds, orange peel and crystallised ginger. Stir until combined, taking care not to break up the flaked almonds.

4. Using a 1 teaspoon measuring spoon, place 24 equal mounds of the mixture onto the lined baking trays, spacing the mounds well apart. (Using a measuring spoon will help you get evenly sized biscuits.)

5. Bake for 10 minutes, until golden brown, then remove from the oven. If you want neat edges, use the round cutter to push any uneven edges into a neat circle, while the florentines are still warm on the baking trays.

6. Leave the florentines to cool on the trays for about 10 minutes, then transfer to a wire rack to cool completely.

7. Melt the chocolate in a bowl set over a pan of gently simmering water. Turn the florentines upside down on the wire rack and spread the chocolate over the bases. Leave to set at room temperature for 5–10 minutes, then use a fork to make ripples in the chocolate. Leave to set completely.

FOR THE SAUCE

300ml double cream
100g light brown soft sugar
75g dark brown soft sugar
100g unsalted butter, cubed
25g 70% dark chocolate,
   chopped
pinch of salt

FOR THE PUDDINGS

175g soft, stoned dates,
   chopped into pea-sized
   pieces
200ml just-boiled water
1 tsp bicarbonate of soda
125g unsalted butter,
   softened
125g light brown soft sugar
50g dark brown soft sugar
2 eggs
150g plain flour
25g cocoa powder
1 tsp baking powder
pinch of salt
100g walnuts, chopped

YOU WILL NEED

15 x 12cm foil containers
   (5cm deep) x 4

Serves
8

Hands on
30 mins

Bake
30 mins

plus chilling

Sticky Toffee Puddings

The addition of chocolate and cocoa to a sticky toffee pudding is a twist on the classic recipe and adds another layer of rich flavour. Baked in foil containers to make them perfect for gifting and each serving two, these sticky toffees make an ideal hug-in-a-pud.

1. Make the sauce. Place the cream, both sugars, and the butter, chocolate and salt in a small pan over a low heat, stirring until the sugar dissolves and the chocolate melts. Bring to the boil, then simmer for 2 minutes, until thickened. Spoon 2 rounded tablespoons of sauce into each foil container, then chill for 30 minutes to firm up.

2. Heat the oven to 180°C/160°C fan/Gas 4.

3. Make the puddings. Place the dates in a heatproof bowl and pour over the just-boiled water. Mix in the bicarbonate of soda and leave to cool for 10 minutes.

4. Meanwhile, beat the butter and both sugars in a stand mixer fitted with the beater, on medium speed for 3–5 minutes, until pale and creamy, scraping down the sides of the bowl from time to time. Add the eggs, one at a time, beating well between each addition.

5. Sift together the flour, cocoa, baking powder and salt into the bowl. Add the date mixture and half the walnuts and mix to combine. Divide the mixture equally between the containers and level the tops. Place on a baking tray and bake for 25 minutes, until well risen and a skewer inserted into the centres comes out clean.

6. Spoon another 1 rounded tablespoon of sauce on top of each pudding, scatter with the remaining nuts and return to the oven for another 5 minutes. Serve immediately with any remaining sauce, and with cream or ice cream; or leave the puddings to cool completely, then cover and chill until ready to reheat (for 20 minutes at 170°C/150°C fan/Gas 3). The puddings freeze well, too.

1 x 150g floury potato
    (such as Maris Piper),
    peeled and halved
500g strong white
    bread flour
7g fast-action dried yeast
1 tsp sea-salt flakes, plus
    extra for sprinkling
325ml lukewarm water
6 tbsp extra-virgin olive oil,
    plus extra for greasing
2 onions, thinly sliced
400g small new potatoes
3 rosemary sprigs,
    needles stripped

YOU WILL NEED
30 x 20cm baking tin
    (at least 4cm deep), oiled

Serves
8–10

Hands on
20 mins
plus rising

Bake
25 mins

Onion and Rosemary Potato Focaccia

There are no fancy techniques involved in making focaccia, so it's super-easy. Adding mashed potato gives soft and bouncy results that keep the bread moister for longer, making it perfect for giving.

1. Boil the potato halves until tender. Drain, then mash until smooth and leave to cool.

2. Tip the flour into a stand mixer fitted with the dough hook, add the yeast and the sea salt and mix to combine. Add the cooled mashed potato, lukewarm water and 3 tablespoons of the olive oil and mix on low speed to combine. Increase the speed to medium and knead for about 5 minutes, until you have a smooth, sticky, elastic dough.

3. Turn out the dough onto a lightly floured work surface, quickly shape into a ball and place in an oiled bowl. Cover and leave to rise for about 1 hour, until doubled in size.

4. Meanwhile, heat 2 tablespoons of the olive oil in a pan, add the onions and cook, stirring occasionally, for about 10 minutes, until soft. Remove from the heat and set aside to cool. Boil the new potatoes in salted water for 10–15 minutes, until just tender. Drain and cool.

5. Turn out the dough into the oiled baking tin and press it to the edges. Cover and prove for 1 hour, or until risen to twice its height.

6. Cut the cooled new potatoes into 2mm-thick slices. Drizzle the remaining 1 tablespoon of extra-virgin olive oil over the dough and gently press your fingertips all over the surface to create dimples.

7. Scatter over sea-salt flakes and arrange the onions and potato slices over the top. Sprinkle with the rosemary. Rest, uncovered, for 20 minutes. Heat the oven to 220°C/200°C fan/Gas 7.

8. Bake the focaccia on the middle shelf for 20–25 minutes, until puffed up and golden brown. Serve warm or at room temperature.

100g blanched almonds
100g blanched hazelnuts
75g unsalted shelled
  pistachios, roughly
  chopped
100g dried figs,
  roughly chopped
100g medjool dates, stoned
  and roughly chopped
2 pieces stem ginger,
  finely chopped,
  plus 2 tbsp syrup
75g dried cherries
50g candied peel
125g plain flour
1 tbsp cocoa powder
1 tsp ground cinnamon
½ tsp ground ginger
¼ tsp ground cloves
¼ tsp ground cardamom
¼ tsp ground nutmeg
¼ tsp freshly ground
  black pepper
pinch of salt
175g runny honey
175g caster sugar
50g 54% dark chocolate,
  roughly chopped
icing sugar, for dusting

YOU WILL NEED
sugar thermometer
23cm springform tin,
  greased, then lined
  (base and sides) with
  baking paper (optional)

Makes
1 cake or 2 logs

Hands on
30 mins

Bake
45 mins

Chocolate Panforte

*A festive Tuscan cake, panforte is dark, dense, chewy and full
of honey, dried fruit, nuts, spices and (in this case) a little dark
chocolate. This recipe makes either 1 large cake or 2 logs – if you
make 2 logs, keep one at home and surprise a friend with the other.
Enjoy it in slices with a coffee (or after dinner, with dessert wine).*

1. Heat the oven to 180°C/160°C fan/Gas 4.

2. Toast the almonds and hazelnuts on a baking tray for about
4 minutes, until light golden. Leave the nuts to cool slightly,
then roughly chop. Reduce the oven to 150°C/130°C fan/Gas 2.

3. Tip the toasted nuts into a large mixing bowl. Mix in the pistachios,
figs, dates, stem ginger, cherries and candied peel. Add the flour,
cocoa, cinnamon, ginger, cloves, cardamom, nutmeg, pepper and
salt and mix well to thoroughly combine.

4. Warm the honey, caster sugar and stem ginger syrup in a small pan
over a low heat for 2–3 minutes, stirring to dissolve the sugar. Increase
the heat slightly and bring the mixture to the boil. Cook for another
2 minutes, or until the mixture reaches 115°C on a sugar thermometer,
then remove from the heat, add the chocolate and stir quickly until
melted and smooth. Pour the melted chocolate mixture into the fruit
and nut mixture and mix well to thoroughly combine.

5. For 1 large panforte, using slightly damp hands, scoop the mixture
into the lined tin and press into an even layer. For logs, lay 2 sheets
of baking paper on your work surface and divide the mixture equally
between them, forming two 18–20cm-long, neat sausage shapes.
Using the paper, roll the panforte up into a tight log and twist the
paper ends to seal. Place in a roasting tin.

6. Bake on the middle shelf for about 45 minutes, until firm, then
remove from the oven. Leave to cool completely (the mixture will firm
up as it cools), then remove from the tin or unwrap. Dust with icing
sugar and serve in slices. Store in an airtight container for 2–3 weeks.

Makes
4

Hands on
1 hour

Bake
20 mins

plus rising

BAKER'S FAVOURITE

Hermine's Ham, Cheese and Chive Couronnes

These brioche couronnes were the first breads I ever made. They have been a real hit as a treat for my colleagues at our monthly office breakfasts, and they are my son's favourites, too.

FOR THE DOUGH
500g strong white
  bread flour
90g caster sugar
10g fine salt
10g fast-action dried yeast
4 eggs, plus 1 extra beaten
  egg for brushing
120ml whole milk, warmed
250g unsalted butter,
  cut into 1cm cubes
  and softened

FOR THE FILLING
½ tsp smoked paprika
300g smoked ham slices
200g Gruyère cheese, grated
10g chives, snipped
freshly ground black pepper

YOU WILL NEED
2 proving bags

1. Make the dough. Place the flour, sugar, salt and yeast in a stand mixer fitted with the dough hook. Crack the eggs into a measuring jug and add enough warm milk to make it up to 290ml. Pour the egg mixture into the dry ingredients and mix on slow speed for 5 minutes, until the dough is smooth and elastic.

2. With the mixer on slow, mix in one quarter of the butter, then continue to add the butter, a quarter at a time, mixing well between each addition, to a soft, shiny dough. Cover the bowl and chill for 4–5 hours, until the dough is firm enough to shape. (Leave it overnight to develop more flavour, if you have time.)

3. Cut the dough into 2 equal pieces. Lightly flour the work surface and roll out each piece to a 45 x 22cm rectangle. Sprinkle the paprika equally on top of each rectangle, then lay the slices of ham on top and sprinkle over the cheese and chives. Season with black pepper.

4. Roll up each piece of dough from the long edge into a tight roll, then cut in half lengthways to give you 4 equal pieces.

5. Take 1 piece of dough and twist it along its length, then form it into a circle and press the ends together to seal. Repeat for the remaining 3 dough pieces. Place the couronnes on 2 baking sheets, then transfer each to a proving bag and leave to prove for about 4–5 hours, until the dough is soft and puffy, and almost doubled in size.

6. Heat the oven to 190°C/170°C fan/Gas 5. Brush the couronnes with the beaten egg. Bake for 20 minutes, until golden brown and cooked through. (Cover with foil after 15 minutes if they become too brown.)

100g coconut oil
75g crunchy peanut butter
100g light brown soft sugar
100g maple syrup
350g rolled oats
  (gluten-free, if required)
75g sultanas
50g flaked almonds
50g coconut flakes
2 tbsp sunflower seeds
2 tbsp pumpkin seeds
1 tbsp sesame seeds
1 tbsp golden linseeds
½ tsp ground cinnamon
75g dried apricots, chopped
  into 1cm pieces
75g soft, stoned dates,
  chopped into 1cm pieces
50g blanched hazelnuts,
  roughly chopped
2 ripe bananas, mashed

YOU WILL NEED
20 x 30cm baking tin
  (4cm deep), oiled, then
  lined (base and sides)
  with baking paper

Makes
20

Hands on
10 mins

Bake
35 mins

Granola Bars

These energy-packed granola bars brim with nuts, seeds, dried fruit, peanut butter and bananas. They are vegan, and if you use gluten-free oats, they can be gluten-free too. Make a batch, wrap them up and hand them out as pick-me-ups on a family hike.

1. Heat the oven to 180°C/160°C fan/Gas 4.

2. In a small saucepan, warm the coconut oil, peanut butter, brown sugar and maple syrup over a low heat, stirring from time to time, until the coconut oil melts. Simmer gently for 30 seconds, then remove from the heat and set aside.

3. Mix together all the remaining ingredients except the mashed bananas in a large mixing bowl.

4. Add the mashed bananas and warm coconut oil mixture to the dry ingredients, then mix well until thoroughly combined. Tip the mixture the into the lined tin and press into an even layer with the back of a spoon. Bake on the middle shelf for 30–35 minutes, until golden.

5. Leave to cool in the tin for 5 minutes, then cut into squares or bars and leave to cool completely before removing from the tin.

FOR THE FILLING
200g minced beef (5% fat)
2 tsp malt vinegar
½ small white onion,
    finely diced
1 spring onion,
    finely chopped
½ red pepper, deseeded
    and finely diced
½ Scotch bonnet chilli,
    deseeded
¼ tsp grated fresh ginger
½ garlic clove, crushed
200g tinned chopped
    tomatoes
2 tsp tomato purée
1 tbsp tomato ketchup
1 tsp demerara sugar
1 tbsp soy sauce
a little gravy browning
    (optional)
good pinch of mixed spice
good pinch of ground
    allspice
good pinch of paprika
good pinch of dried thyme
salt and freshly ground
    black pepper

FOR THE PASTRY
100g unsalted butter, cubed
80g white vegetable
    shortening
300g plain flour
2 tsp ground turmeric
½ tsp yellow food-colouring
    paste (optional)
1 tbsp lemon juice

YOU WILL NEED
12cm round cutter
    (or use a saucer)

Makes
12

Hands on
1½ hours

Bake
25 mins

plus chilling

BAKER'S FAVOURITE

Loriea's Jamaican Beef Patties

I remember eating these Jamaican patties from a young age. For me, they are a little taste of the kindness of home. After moving to the UK, the patties were one of the first things I tried making for my family, even while I was still at school. The unique blend of spices and aromas should give everyone a small bite of Jamaica.

1. Make the filling. Place the minced beef on a plate, add ½ teaspoon of the vinegar and mix well. Place the mixture in a sieve and run it under the cold tap for a few seconds. Press out as much moisture as possible, then pat dry with kitchen paper.

2. Place the beef in a medium saucepan with another ½ teaspoon of the vinegar and dry fry until browned and most of the moisture has evaporated. Add the onion, spring onion, red pepper, chilli, ginger and garlic, and fry over a medium heat for 5 minutes, then add all the remaining filling ingredients. Bring to the boil, reduce the heat and simmer for 30 minutes, stirring occasionally, or until most of the liquid has evaporated. Season with salt and pepper to taste, then spread out on a plate and leave to cool.

3. Make the pastry. Mix the butter and vegetable shortening together with a wooden spoon until smooth. Place 45g of the fat in a food processor and chill the remainder. Add the flour, turmeric and colouring (if using), to the processor and blend to fine crumbs.

4. Add the lemon juice and 120ml water and pulse until the mixture clumps together. Turn out the dough, gather it into a ball and knead for 2 minutes, until smooth. Wrap and chill for 30 minutes.

5. Turn out the chilled dough onto a lightly floured work surface. Roll it out into a roughly 30 x 20cm rectangle. Cut the remaining chilled fat into three 45g portions.

Continues overleaf

6. Dot one portion of the fat evenly over two thirds of the pastry, leaving the top third clean. Fold the top third down, then fold the bottom third over as if folding a business letter. Press with a rolling pin to seal the edges.

7. Give the pastry a quarter turn and roll out into a rectangle again, repeat with the fat and fold once more. Repeat for a third time, rolling out the pastry and using the remaining fat. Roll and fold one more time, then wrap and chill the pastry for a further 30 minutes.

8. Heat the oven to 200°C/180°C fan/Gas 6.

9. Halve the dough and roll out thinly to a roughly 36 x 20cm rectangle. Using the pastry cutter (or saucer), cut out six 12cm pastry discs, then repeat with the other half of the dough, re-rolling the trimmings if necessary until you have 12 discs.

10. Divide the filling equally between the rounds, spooning it on one side of each piece of pastry and leaving a border all the way around.

11. Dampen the pastry border with water, then fold the dough over the filling and press the edges together with a fork to seal. Make 2 small slits in the top of each patty and place on a baking tray. Bake for 20–25 minutes, until golden brown. Serve hot or cold.

1 small–medium sweet
    potato, peeled and
    cut into even chunks
100g peanut butter,
    crunchy or smooth
1 egg, lightly beaten
25g dried cranberries,
    roughly chopped
2 tsp finely chopped fresh
    parsley or 1 tsp dried
25g porridge oats
175g wholemeal flour

YOU WILL NEED
8–9cm bone-shaped cutter
large baking sheet,
    greased, then lined
    with baking paper

Makes
25

Hands on
20 mins

Bake
15 mins

Good-dog Biscuits

No chapter featuring acts of kindness could be complete without a treat for your favourite pooch. Do check that your pet doesn't have any allergies before feeding them anything other than their regular food, though, and always check the labels of the recipe ingredients – for example, some brands of peanut butter contain xylitol, which is toxic to dogs. Cookie cutters come in all sorts of dog-themed shapes, but what hound doesn't sit earnestly for a bone?

1. Heat the oven to 170°C/150°C fan/Gas 3.

2. Steam or boil the sweet potato until tender. Drain well, mash until smooth and leave to cool.

3. Weigh the mashed sweet potato and spoon 125g into a mixing bowl – you can freeze any leftover for another time, or stir it into soup or hummus (for humans, obviously).

4. Mix the peanut butter and egg into the sweet potato. Add the dried cranberries, fresh or dried parsley and the oats and mix again. Add the flour and, using your hands, mix until thoroughly combined.

5. Roll out the mixture on a lightly floured work surface until about 2–3mm thick. Using the cutter, stamp out as many shapes as you can, re-rolling the trimmings as necessary (you should get about 25 bone shapes). Arrange the dog biscuits on the lined baking sheet.

6. Bake the biscuits on the middle shelf for about 15 minutes, or until crisp and starting to turn pale brown around the edges. Leave to cool on the baking sheet – they will crisp further as they cool. Store in an airtight box or tin and serve as a treat for good behaviour!

Photography overleaf

CHAPTER TWO

Little Bakers

Recipes

ROCKY ROAD

STEAMED BUN PANDAS

CHEESE TWISTS

BUTTON MERINGUES

PAUL'S RAINBOW-COLOURED BAGELS

COOKIE BUNTING

MINI PIZZAS

PRUE'S COCONUT MACAROONS

BUTTERFLY CAKES

DAVE'S TRIPLE CHOCOLATE BROWNIES

CHEESE GOUGÈRES

THUMBPRINT BISCUITS

MALT LOAF

FOR THE BISCUIT
75g plain flour
50g plain wholemeal flour
¼ tsp bicarbonate of soda
pinch of salt
35g light brown soft sugar
75g unsalted butter,
   cubed and chilled
1 tbsp whole milk

FOR THE ROCKY ROAD
200g milk chocolate,
   roughly chopped,
   plus an extra 50g,
   melted, for drizzling
100g 54% dark chocolate,
   roughly chopped
75g unsalted butter, cubed
1 rounded tbsp golden syrup
75g glacé cherries, halved
50g raisins
75g mini marshmallows

YOU WILL NEED
20cm square traybake
   tin, greased, then lined
   (base and sides) with
   baking paper

Makes
16-20

Hands on
30 mins

Bake
18 mins

plus chilling

Rocky Road

Biscuits, marshmallows, raisins and sticky glacé cherries all held together with chocolate – rocky road has it all, and is so easy and fun to put together, it's practically child's play. The best thing about this version, though, is the delicious homemade biscuit.

1. Heat the oven to 180°C/160°C fan/Gas 4.

2. Make the biscuit. Sift both types of flour, the bicarbonate of soda and salt into a large mixing bowl. Add the sugar and mix to combine. Using your fingertips, rub the butter into the dry ingredients until there are no flecks of butter remaining and the mixture is the texture of coarse sand.

3. Make a well in the centre, add the milk and, using a palette knife, bring the dough together into clumps. Very gently knead the dough until you have a neat, smooth ball.

4. Lightly dust the work surface with flour. Flatten the dough into a rough square, then roll out into a neat 20cm square. Place into the lined tin, pressing the dough out evenly to fill the tin, then prick with a fork. Bake for about 18 minutes, until it starts to turn golden brown at the edges. Remove from the oven and turn out onto a wire rack to cool – it will firm and crisp as it cools. Grease and re-line the tin.

5. Make the rocky road. Melt both chocolates, and the butter and golden syrup in a heatproof bowl set over a pan of barely simmering water. Stir until smooth and remove from the heat.

6. While the chocolate is melting, break the cooled biscuit into bite-sized chunks. Place in a large bowl with the glacé cherries, raisins and almost all the marshmallows. Add the melted chocolate mixture and stir until combined. Spoon into the lined tin and spread level with a palette knife. Press the remaining marshmallows into the top, leave to cool, then cover and chill for about 1 hour, until firm.

7. Remove the rocky road from the tin. Drizzle with the extra chocolate, and, using a large, sharp knife, cut into 16–20 squares.

FOR THE DOUGH
375g plain flour, plus
    extra for dusting
7g fast-action dried yeast
20g caster sugar
2 tbsp vegetable oil
175ml lukewarm water
black food-colouring paste

YOU WILL NEED
15 squares of baking paper,
    each measuring 10 x 10cm
small piping nozzle or 1cm
    round cutter
steamer

Steamed Bun Pandas

These fluffy balls of mantou dough can be served up vegan or non-vegan and savoury or sweet – filled with shredded tofu, or pulled pork or duck, perhaps; or with honey or vegan chocolate sauce for dipping. The Japanese trend is to make sweeter dough shaped like animals or clouds, making them a fun way to get children involved in the kitchen.

1. Place the flour, yeast, sugar and oil into the bowl of a stand mixer fitted with the dough hook. Add the warm water and mix, on slow speed for 4–5 minutes, until the dough is smooth.

2. Tip out the dough onto a lightly floured surface and roll into a 5cm-diameter sausage measuring 45cm long. Cut the sausage into 16 equal pieces of about 35g each.

3. Set 1 piece aside for the eyes, ears and mouths and shape the remaining 15 pieces into neat balls.

4. Place each dough ball on a square of baking paper, rounded side up, and transfer to a baking tray, spacing the balls well apart. Cover lightly with oiled cling film and leave to rise for about 30 minutes or more, until doubled in size (how long this takes will depend on the ambient temperature in your kitchen).

5. While the balls are rising, pull off a pea-sized piece from the 16th ball of dough and set aside. Colour the remaining dough using the black food-colouring paste, kneading to an even, strong black colour.

6. Halve the black dough and roll one half into 15 pea-sized balls. Cut the balls in half to make 30 little semi-spherical ears.

7. Place 2 ears on each of the balls of dough, lifting the cling film so you can attach them while the dough is rising.

8. Roll out the remaining black dough thinly and cut out 30 eyes using the end of the piping nozzle or the cutter.

Continues overleaf

9. Lift away the trimmings of dough between the circles, then, using the cutter again, cut the edge off each circle to turn the eyes into oval shapes. The little semi-circle trimming will become the mouths.

10. Brushing with a little water to ensure the features stick, place a pair of eyes on each ball of dough, add the little semi-circle trimmings for the mouths and, from the scraps, roll a tiny black nose for each face. From the reserved white dough, roll tiny balls for the pupils.

11. Once the white dough balls have risen to double their size (this may take as long or longer than it takes you to make the faces), in batches place the pandas, sitting on their squares of paper, into a steamer.

12. Cover with a tight-fitting lid and steam the buns for 15 minutes, until the dough is cooked and feels squishy but does not leave an impression when you press it with a finger.

13. Leave the buns to cool a little, then serve hot.

FOR THE ROUGH
PUFF PASTRY
300g plain flour, sifted
½ tsp salt
200g unsalted butter,
    thoroughly chilled
150–170ml ice-cold water
1 tsp lemon juice or white
    wine vinegar

FOR THE FILLING
3 tbsp Marmite
250g Cheddar cheese,
    finely grated
1–2 tbsp whole milk,
    for glazing
2 tbsp poppy seeds

YOU WILL NEED
2 baking sheets,
    greased, then lined
    with baking paper

Makes
32

Hands on
30 mins

Bake
18 mins

plus chilling

Cheese Twists

A brilliant introduction to rough puff pastry (and the process of lamination), these crisp, cheesy twists are great fun to make – and a good test of patience! Even though rough puff is quicker and simpler to make than full puff, it still needs thoroughly chilling between repeated roll-and-folds.

1. Make the rough puff pastry. Tip the flour and salt into a large mixing bowl. Grate the butter into the flour, using the coarse side of a box grater. Using your hands, lightly mix the butter into the flour, just enough to separate and coat the butter in flour.

2. Stir 150ml of the ice-cold water and the lemon juice or vinegar into the flour mixture with a palette knife, mixing gently to bring the dough together – add up to 4 teaspoons extra water, if needed, until you have a rough dough.

3. Turn out the dough onto a lightly floured work surface and flatten it into a neat square. Using a rolling pin in sharp tapping motions, roll out the dough into a 36 x 12cm rectangle with one of the short sides closest to you.

4. Neatly fold the bottom third of the pastry up to the middle and the top third down over it to cover, as if you were folding a business letter – the dough should be a neat square with three layers. Turn the dough through 90° clockwise (a quarter turn).

5. Roll out the dough into a rectangle as before. Repeat the folding, trying to keep the sides as neat as possible. Carefully wrap in cling film or baking paper and chill for 1 hour.

6. Lightly flour the work surface again, then roll out (as before), fold the pastry and chill it again. Roll and fold for a final time, then cover and chill for 2–4 hours before use.

Continues overleaf

7. Lightly flour the work surface and cut the dough in half. Cover and chill one half while you roll the other half out to a neat 35cm square.

8. Gently warm the Marmite in a microwave for 10 seconds until slightly runny. Using a pastry brush, dab half of it all over the top of the pastry – it will not brush smoothly, but don't worry.

9. Scatter half the grated cheese evenly over the bottom half of the pastry square, then fold the top half down over it to cover.

10. Lightly roll the pastry, cheese and Marmite sandwich together, brush with milk and scatter with poppy seeds. Using a long, sharp knife, cut into 16 strips, each about 2cm wide. (Cook's perks: bake and eat any trimmings.)

11. Twist each pastry strip three times along its length and arrange the strips on the lined baking sheet. Chill these twists while you repeat with the second half of the pastry. Then, chill all the cheese twists for another 30 minutes.

12. Meanwhile, heat the oven to 200°C/180°C fan/Gas 6.

13. Bake the cheese and Marmite twists for about 18 minutes, until the they are crisp and golden. Remove from the oven and leave to cool and crisp up on the baking sheets.

3 large egg whites
pinch of salt
175g caster sugar
pink, yellow and green
    food-colouring pastes

YOU WILL NEED
medium piping bag fitted
    with a medium open
    star nozzle
2 large baking sheets,
    lined with baking paper

Gluten Free

Makes
80

Hands on
30 mins

Bake
40 mins

Button Meringues

These super-pretty meringues are easy to make with children.
Keep an eye as you add the food colouring, remembering that
a little goes a long way. Serve them plain or with ice cream, or
sandwiched with whipped cream, or use them to decorate cakes.

1. Heat the oven to 120°C/100°C fan/Gas ¾.

2. Tip the egg whites into the bowl of a stand mixer fitted with the whisk, add the salt and whisk on medium speed until the egg whites almost hold stiff peaks.

3. Add the sugar, 1 tablespoon at a time, whisking well between each addition until the mixture is smooth and the sugar is thoroughly incorporated. Continue whisking until you have added all the sugar and the meringue is bright white, silky smooth and very stiff.

4. Divide the meringue equally between 3 bowls. Using a wooden skewer, add a tiny amount of pink food colouring to one bowl, then mix well to evenly distribute the colour throughout the mixture. Add yellow food colouring to the second bowl and green to the third, mixing to combine each time.

5. Spoon the pink meringue into the piping bag and twist the top to seal. Pipe small 'kisses', each about the size of a large grape, onto the lined baking sheets in neat lines and leaving a little space between each meringue.

6. When you've used up the pink meringue, spoon the yellow meringue into the same bag and pipe more kisses. Repeat with the green. (You could use three piping bags and nozzles – one for each colour – but piping the different colours one after the other from the same piping bag gives the first few meringues each time lovely unicorn or rainbow stripes.)

7. Bake the meringues for 40 minutes, until crisp and dry. Turn off the oven and leave them inside to cool completely before serving.

375g strong white
  bread flour
5g fast-action dried yeast
2 tsp caster sugar
1 tsp fine salt
240ml lukewarm water
red, orange, yellow,
  green and blue
  food-colouring paste
1 tsp bicarbonate of soda

YOU WILL NEED
5 mixing bowls, greased
  with sunflower oil
2 baking sheets,
  greased, then lined
  with baking paper
2 proving bags

Makes
6

Hands on
1 hour

plus rising

Bake
30 mins

JUDGE'S RECIPE

Paul's Rainbow-coloured Bagels

What could be more magical than making a rainbow? We've chosen rainbow hues for this dough, but feel free to experiment with your own favourite colours to make the bagels your own.

1. Place the flour in a mixing bowl, add the yeast to one side and the sugar and salt to the other. Add three-quarters of the water and turn the mixture with your fingers. Add the remaining water, a little at a time, until all the flour is incorporated and you have a rough dough.

2. Tip the dough onto a lightly floured work surface and knead for 5–10 minutes, to a soft, smooth ball.

3. Divide the dough into 5 equal pieces and cover with a damp tea towel. Working with 1 piece of dough at a time, turn each into a different colour. Add 3 pea-sized drops of food colouring onto the dough, then fold it up and around the colouring. Knead to an even colour, adding more food colouring, a drop at a time, until bright. Place the coloured dough into a greased bowl.

4. Repeat with the other 4 pieces of dough until you have 5 brightly coloured portions of dough. Cover each bowl with a tea towel and leave to rise for about 45 minutes–1 hour, until doubled in size.

5. Turn out the red dough onto a lightly floured work surface and, using a rolling pin, roll out to a 20 x 12cm rectangle. Set aside. Turn out the orange dough onto a lightly floured work surface and roll out also to a 20 x 12cm rectangle. Place the orange rectangle of dough neatly on top of the red.

6. Repeat with the yellow, green and blue doughs, rolling each one out and placing on top of one another, until you have a stack of 5 layers of dough, red at the bottom, then orange, yellow, green and blue.

Continues overleaf

7. Cut the stacked dough into six 20 x 2cm-wide slices, slicing down through the layers, so each strip has 5 layers of colour.

8. To shape the bagels, lay one of the stacked dough strips on your work surface and place the palm of your hands at each end. Simultaneously, gently move your right hand forwards and your left hand backwards to twist the dough into a rope about 26cm long. Pinch the ends together to form a circle and gently roll the join backwards and forwards to seal. Repeat with all the strips.

9. Place the bagels on the lined baking sheets, then place in proving bags and leave to prove for 20 minutes, until risen and puffed up.

10. Heat the oven to 200°C/180°C fan/Gas 6.

11. Bring a large saucepan of water to the boil. Add the bicarbonate of soda (this helps to form the shine and chewy texture of the crust).

12. Plunge the bagels, 2 or 3 at a time depending on the size of your pan, into the boiling water. Cook for 30 seconds on each side, until the bagels puff up and the shape sets. Using a slotted spoon, remove each bagel from the water and transfer back to the baking sheet.

13. Bake the bagels for 25–30 minutes, until cooked through. Remove from the oven and transfer to a wire rack to cool.

Makes
30 biscuits

Hands on
2 hours
plus chilling

Bake
24 mins

FOR THE SHORTBREAD

225g unsalted butter,
   softened
150g icing sugar, sifted
1 egg, lightly beaten
1 tsp vanilla paste
350g plain flour
½ tsp baking powder
pinch of salt

FOR THE ROYAL ICING

500g icing sugar
2 egg whites
4 different food-colouring
   pastes, in your choice
   of colours

YOU WILL NEED

2 baking sheets,
   greased, then lined
   with baking paper
5 small paper piping bags
ribbon or string for
   threading

Cookie Bunting

Who needs fabric bunting when you can make it from cookies? These flag-shaped shortbread biscuits will need lots of input from little helpers – to bake, ice and string together. Ice three or four biscuits in one colour at a time (so that the icing stays workable) before you move on to the next. Make the biscuits the day before serving to give the icing time to harden up properly.

1. Make the shortbread. Beat the butter and icing sugar together in a stand mixer fitted with the beater, on medium speed for 3–5 minutes, until pale and creamy, scraping down the sides of the bowl from time to time.

2. Add the egg, a little at a time, beating well after each addition. Add the vanilla paste and mix again.

3. Sift together the flour, baking powder and salt into the bowl and mix until smooth (don't over-mix or the biscuits will be tough). Flatten the dough into a neat rectangle, then wrap and chill for about 2 hours, until firm.

4. Lightly flour the work surface. Roll out half the dough into a 30 x 22cm rectangle, about 2mm thick. Cut the rectangle into two long strips, then into triangles, each about 10cm long. Arrange on the lined baking sheets. Repeat with the remaining dough, re-rolling the trimmings, to give about 30 triangle-shaped biscuits.

5. Using a wooden skewer, make a hole in each corner of the short side of the triangles to thread through the ribbon or string after baking. Chill the biscuits for 15 minutes.

6. Heat the oven to 170°C/150°C fan/Gas 3.

7. Bake the biscuits in batches on the middle shelf for 10–12 minutes each, until firm and turning golden at the edges. Cool on the baking sheets for a few minutes, then push the skewer through the holes again to re-open, and transfer to a wire rack to cool completely.

Continues overleaf

8. To decorate, make the royal icing. Sift the icing sugar into the bowl of a stand mixer fitted with the whisk. Starting on a slow speed, add the egg whites and 2 tablespoons of water. Increase to medium speed and whisk for 1–2 minutes, until smooth and thick, adding more water, a little at a time, until the icing holds a firm ribbon trail when you lift the whisk.

9. Divide the icing equally between 5 bowls and add a different food colouring – in tiny increments and mixing thoroughly between each addition – to four of the bowls, leaving the fifth bowl white. Bear in mind that the colours often become stronger over time.

10. Scoop 1–2 tablespoons of each colour icing into separate piping bags, twist the tops to seal and snip off the ends into fine points. Cover the bowls to prevent the remaining icing drying out.

11. Pipe a neat, continuous line of icing around the edge of each shortbread triangle and around the holes in the top corners. Leave the icing to dry and harden for about 30 minutes. Store the piping bags in an airtight box in the meantime to prevent the icing drying out.

12. Add a little more water to the icing in each bowl until you reach the consistency of runny honey. Working in small batches and using a teaspoon, spoon the icing into the middle of each shortbread triangle, then spread out with the back of the spoon to neatly fill the outline. Leave to set slightly before decorating. Using contrasting colours, pipe fine lines or polka dots onto the icing.

13. Repeat with the remaining shortbreads and icing. Leave for at least 4 hours (but preferably overnight) for the icing to set firm before threading the biscuits onto ribbons or pretty string to turn them into edible bunting.

FOR THE DOUGH
250g strong white
bread flour
250g type '00' flour
7g fast-action dried yeast
1 tsp caster sugar
1 tsp salt
2 tbsp olive oil
325ml lukewarm water,
plus extra if needed

FOR THE TOMATO SAUCE
400g passata
½ tsp dried oregano
pinch of caster sugar,
if needed
salt and freshly ground
black pepper

**FOR THE TOPPINGS
(CHOOSE FROM)**
125g mozzarella ball,
drained and diced
thinly sliced pepperoni
or chorizo
thinly sliced ham
sliced black olives
sweetcorn kernels
sliced cherry tomatoes
anchovies
cooked spinach
micro basil leaves,
to finish

YOU WILL NEED
2 baking sheets,
greased, then lined
with baking paper

Makes
16

Hands on
40 mins

plus rising

Bake
12 mins

Mini Pizzas

These mini pizzas are the perfect size for little hands to make and shape and a fun way to introduce children to the world of making bread – set up a pizza kitchen on your worktop and let everyone choose their own toppings. (Almost) anything goes!

1. Tip both types of flour into a large bowl (or the bowl of a stand mixer fitted with the dough hook). Add the yeast, sugar and salt and mix well to combine. Make a well in the centre, add the olive oil and the lukewarm water and mix well to combine. Add 1 tablespoon more water if the mixture looks too dry – it needs to be soft and slightly sticky. Knead for about 10 minutes, until smooth and elastic.

2. Shape the dough into a ball and place in a large, oiled bowl. Cover and leave to rise at room temperature for about 1 hour, until the dough has doubled in size.

3. Meanwhile, make the tomato sauce. Pour the passata into a small pan, add the oregano, set over a low–medium heat and bring to the boil. Reduce the heat and simmer for 3–4 minutes, stirring from time to time, until slightly thickened. Season with salt and pepper, and add a pinch of caster sugar if needed to balance the flavour. Leave to cool.

4. Heat the oven to 220°C/200°C fan/Gas 7.

5. Turn out the dough onto a lightly floured work surface and knead for 30 seconds to knock out any large air bubbles. Cut the dough into 16 equal portions. Shape the portions into balls and leave to rest for 5 minutes.

6. Roll or stretch out the dough balls into neat rounds, each about 12cm in diameter, and arrange on the lined baking sheets. Spread 2 teaspoons of the tomato sauce onto each pizza, leaving a small border. Scatter over the mozzarella and your choice of toppings.

7. Bake on the middle shelf for about 12 minutes, swapping the trays around halfway, until the pizzas are bubbling and the dough crust is risen and golden. Scatter with basil leaves to finish.

FOR THE MANGO CURD
75g mango purée
2 tsp caster sugar
1 egg
2 egg yolks
2 tsp lime juice
50g unsalted butter, cubed

FOR THE MACAROONS
350g sweetened
    shredded coconut
240g condensed milk
½ tsp almond extract
2 tbsp rice flour
2 egg whites
¼ tsp salt
100g 54% dark chocolate,
    broken into pieces

YOU WILL NEED
6cm round cutter or a
    similar-sized glass
2 sheets edible rice paper
baking sheet, greased, then
    lined with baking paper
large piping bag fitted with
    a large open star nozzle
small piping bag fitted with
    a small writing nozzle

Gluten
Free

Makes
12

Hands on
1 hour

Bake
30 mins

Prue's Coconut Macaroons

*Coconut macaroons are naturally gluten-free, making them a
brilliant sweet treat for all the family. Crispy on the outside
and chewy in the centres, there are two flavours here:
chocolate and zingy mango curd.*

1. Make the mango curd. Pour the mango purée into a small heatproof
bowl and add the sugar, egg and egg yolks. Using a balloon whisk,
whisk the sugar and egg mixture together until well combined,
then whisk in the lime juice.

2. Place the bowl over a pan of simmering water and cook over a
medium heat, stirring with a rubber spatula for 5–7 minutes until the
mixture has thickened and coats the back of a spoon. Remove from
the heat, transfer to a clean bowl and leave to cool for 5 minutes.

3. Add the butter a little at a time, stirring between each addition,
until smooth. Pour into a sterilised jar, cover and leave to cool, then
chill until set. (This will make more than you need, but you can store
the remainder in the fridge for up to 3 weeks and enjoy on toast.)

4. Heat the oven to 150°C/130°C fan/Gas 2.

5. Make the macaroons. Using the cutter (or glass) as a guide, draw
12 circles, each 6cm in diameter, on the rice paper. Cut out the circles
and arrange on the lined baking sheet, evenly spaced apart.

6. Tip the shredded coconut into the bowl of a food processor
and blitz for 1–2 minutes, until the flakes are the size of desiccated
coconut. Add the condensed milk, almond extract and rice flour
and pulse until well combined. Transfer to a bowl.

7. Using an electric hand whisk, whisk the egg whites and salt together to stiff (but not dry) peaks. Carefully fold the egg whites into the coconut mixture.

8. Spoon half the mixture into the large piping bag fitted with a large open star nozzle and twist the top to seal.

9. Pipe a ring of the coconut mixture around the edge of six of the rice-paper circles, leaving a space in the middle. Pipe a small amount of the mixture into the space, just enough to cover the rice paper, but leaving an indent large enough for 1 teaspoon of the mango curd.

10. Spoon 1 tablespoon of coconut mixture onto each of the remaining 6 discs of rice paper and flatten with your fingers to make flat rounds. Place a piece of chocolate in the centre of each of these coconut circles, then top with a heaped tablespoon of the coconut mixture. Using your hands, shape and smooth the tops and sides of each one into a dome, so the chocolate is hidden inside.

11. Bake all the macaroons for 25–30 minutes, turning the baking sheet halfway through, until the tops and edges are golden.

12. Remove from the oven and leave to cool on the baking sheet for 5 minutes, then transfer to a wire rack and leave to cool completely. The macaroons will crisp up and harden on the outsides as they cool.

13. To decorate, melt the remaining chocolate in a heatproof bowl set over a pan of barely simmering water, stirring occasionally. Remove from the heat and leave to cool slightly.

14. Spoon the chocolate into the small piping bag fitted with the writing nozzle and pipe fine lines across the chocolate macaroons, then leave to set.

15. Using a teaspoon, place a small amount of the mango curd into the centre of each macaroon ring before serving.

Photography overleaf

FOR THE CAKES

175g unsalted butter, softened
175g caster sugar
3 eggs, beaten
1 tsp vanilla extract
175g self-raising flour, sifted
pinch of salt
2 tbsp whole milk

FOR THE BUTTERCREAM

100g unsalted butter, softened
200g icing sugar, sifted, plus extra for dusting
1 tsp vanilla extract

TO FILL & DECORATE

6 rounded tsp raspberry jam or lemon curd
assorted sprinkles or fresh berries

YOU WILL NEED

12-hole muffin tray, lined with 12 cupcake cases
small piping bag fitted with a medium open star nozzle (optional)

Makes
12

Hands on
30 mins

Bake
20 mins

Butterfly Cakes

With no complicated mixing nor fancy decoration, and ready in under an hour, butterfly cakes are the perfect entry into the world of baking for little helpers. If you like, replace 25g of the flour with cocoa powder for chocolate cakes.

1. Heat the oven to 180°C/160°C fan/Gas 4.

2. Make the cakes. Beat the butter and sugar in a stand mixer fitted with the beater, on medium speed for 3–5 minutes, until pale and creamy, scraping down the sides of the bowl from time to time.

3. Add the eggs, a little at a time, beating well between each addition. Add the vanilla extract and beat again.

4. Add the flour, salt and milk to the bowl and beat until the mixture is glossy and smooth.

5. Divide the mixture equally between the cupcake cases. Bake on the middle shelf for 18–20 minutes, until golden, well risen and a skewer inserted into the centres comes out clean. Remove from the oven and leave to stand in the tray for 3–4 minutes, then remove from the tray and place on a wire rack to cool completely.

6. Meanwhile make the buttercream. Beat the butter until pale and creamy. Gradually, add the icing sugar and continue beating until fluffy. Add the vanilla extract and mix to combine.

7. Using a small, sharp knife, cut a cone-shaped hole out of the top of each cupcake and set aside the cuttings. Spoon ½ teaspoon of jam or lemon curd into the hole in each cake, then pipe or spoon a swirl of buttercream on top to fill the hole.

8. Cut each of the reserved cake cones in half and place them on top of the buttercream, to make butterfly wings.

9. Lightly dust the cakes with icing sugar and scatter with sprinkles or top with fresh berries.

375g unsalted butter, cubed
375g 54% dark chocolate,
    roughly chopped
6 eggs
350g light muscovado sugar
225g plain flour
½ tsp crushed sea salt
150g white chocolate,
    roughly chopped
150g milk chocolate,
    roughly chopped

TO DECORATE
25g 70% dark chocolate
¼ tsp sunflower or
    coconut oil

YOU WILL NEED
33 x 23cm traybake tin,
    greased, then base-lined
    with baking paper
small paper piping bag
    (optional)

BAKER'S FAVOURITE

Dave's Triple-chocolate Brownies

Young or old, everyone loves my triple-chocolate brownies. Above all, they are my partner's favourite dessert – in fact, they are pretty much the only dessert she eats! They are delicious just as they are, but I love serving them warm with ice cream (or clotted cream, as a dessert) and a sprinkling of homemade honeycomb on the side.

1. Heat the oven to 180°C/160°C fan/Gas 4.

2. Melt the butter in a medium pan over a low heat, stirring occasionally. Add the dark chocolate, remove from the heat and stir until melted and smooth. Leave to cool slightly.

3. Crack the eggs into a medium mixing bowl and, using a balloon whisk, mix in the sugar until combined. Gradually, pour the melted chocolate mixture into the egg mixture, whisking until smooth.

4. Using a wooden spoon, fold in the flour and salt, then stir in the white and milk chocolate until evenly distributed.

5. Pour the mixture into the lined tin. Bake for 25 minutes for very gooey brownies, 27 minutes for slightly gooey (easier to cut into nice slices) and 30 minutes for slightly cakey brownies. Leave to cool, then carefully remove from the tin.

6. To decorate, melt the chocolate and sunflower or coconut oil in a small heatproof bowl set over a pan of barely simmering water. Stir until smooth, then remove from the heat.

7. Using a teaspoon, drizzle the melted chocolate over the brownies. (For a neater effect, pour the chocolate into a piping bag, twist the top and snip the end into a fine point, then drizzle in swirls over the top.) Leave the topping to set, then cut into 12 squares to serve.

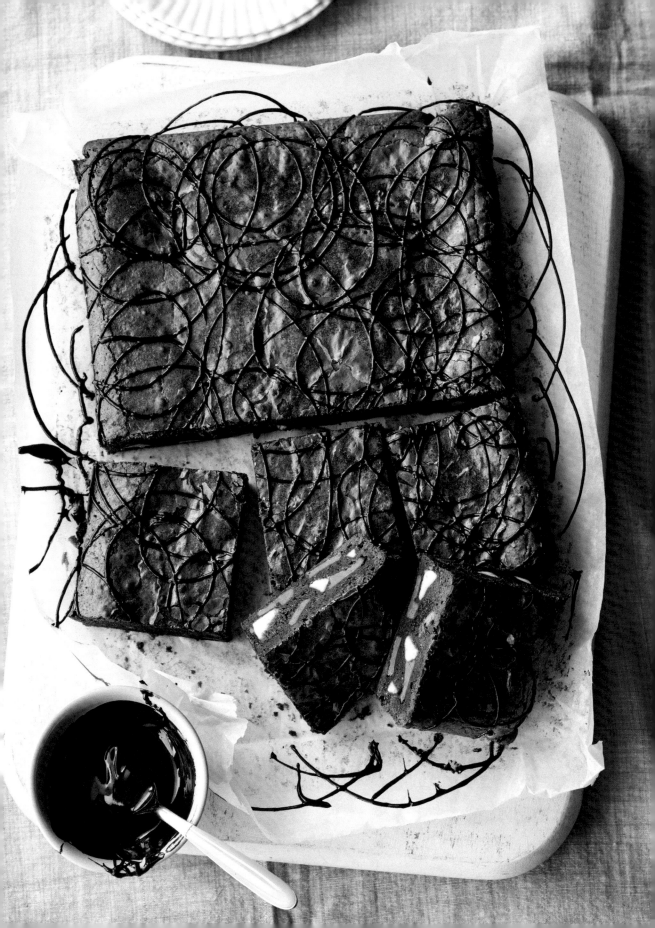

FOR THE TOMATO SAUCE
1 garlic clove, crushed
1 tbsp olive oil
small pinch of dried oregano
small pinch of dried chilli
   flakes (optional)
400g tin of chopped
   tomatoes
pinch of caster sugar
pinch of salt
freshly ground black pepper

FOR THE GOUGÈRES
90g gluten-free plain flour
¼ tsp xanthan gum
¼ tsp dried English
   mustard powder
60g unsalted butter, cubed
pinch of cayenne pepper
3 eggs, lightly beaten
75g Cheddar cheese,
   finely grated
25g Parmesan cheese,
   finely grated

FOR THE FILLING
250g full-fat cream cheese
2 tbsp crème fraîche
2 tbsp snipped chives

YOU WILL NEED
2 baking sheets,
   greased, then lined
   with baking paper
medium piping bag fitted
   with a medium plain nozzle

Makes
about 35

Hands on
40 mins

Bake
22 mins

Cheese Gougères

*These bite-sized cheesy puffs are easy for little bakers to make –
just take care near the oven and hob. This recipe is gluten-free, but
if you prefer to make the gougères using regular flour, simply swap
in 100g plain flour and leave out the xanthan gum. You can make
them vegetarian if you use veggie-friendly Parmesan.*

1. Make the tomato sauce. Tip the garlic into a small pan, add the
olive oil, oregano, and the chilli flakes (if using). Set the pan over
a low–medium heat and cook for about 1 minute, stirring, until the
garlic smells aromatic. Add the chopped tomatoes and continue to
cook, stirring frequently, for about 10 minutes, until thickened slightly.

2. Blend the sauce with a hand-held stick blender until smooth.
Stir in the sugar and season with salt and pepper.

3. Heat the oven to 200°C/180°C fan/Gas 6.

4. Make the gougères. Sift together the gluten-free flour, xanthan
gum and mustard powder in a mixing bowl.

5. Pour 150ml water into a medium pan. Add the butter and melt
over a medium heat, making sure the water doesn't boil. As soon as
the butter melts, bring the mixture to a rolling boil. Working quickly,
slide the pan off the heat, add the flour mixture and beat vigorously
until the mixture is smooth and cleanly leaves the sides of the pan.
Add the cayenne, and season with salt and pepper. Scoop the mixture
into a medium bowl and leave to cool for 5 minutes.

6. Gradually, add the eggs, 1 tablespoon at a time, beating well
between each addition, until the mixture is thick and drops off the
spoon. The mixture may not look totally smooth, and it will be thicker
than regular choux pastry. Add all but 1 rounded tablespoon of the
grated Cheddar and all of the Parmesan and mix to combine.

Continues overleaf

7. Using a dessertspoon, drop about 35 small, neat mounds of dough (each no bigger than a walnut) onto the lined baking sheets, leaving a little space between each one, and scatter with the reserved cheese. Bake on the middle shelves for about 20–22 minutes, until well risen and light golden brown.

8. Push a wooden skewer into the underside of each gougère to allow the steam to escape and return to the oven for a further 1 minute. Remove from the oven and leave to cool to room temperature.

9. Meanwhile, make the filling. Combine the cream cheese, crème fraîche and chives in a small bowl. Spoon the mixture into the piping bag fitted with a plain nozzle and twist the top to seal.

10. Using the tip of a sharp knife, pierce a hole in the bottom of each gougère. Insert the end of the piping nozzle and pipe the cheese mixture into each bun to fill.

11. Serve immediately with the tomato sauce for dipping.

FOR THE SHORTBREAD
200g unsalted butter,
  softened
100g caster sugar
25g icing sugar, sifted
2 egg yolks
1 tsp vanilla extract
275g plain flour, sifted
pinch of salt

FOR THE CRUMBLE
100g plain flour
75g unsalted butter,
  cubed and chilled
50g caster sugar
25g light brown soft sugar

FOR THE FILLING
12–18 tsp raspberry jam,
  lemon curd or chocolate
  hazelnut spread or
  24 giant milk
  chocolate buttons

YOU WILL NEED
12–hole muffin trays x 2,
  greased

Makes
24

Hands on
30 mins

Bake
18 mins

plus chilling

Thumbprint Biscuits

A cross between a buttery shortbread and a jam tart, these biscuits are ideal for pleasing the whole family – jam, lemon curd, chocolate spread or giant chocolate buttons are all delicious fillings. Make a selection and everyone can have a go at constructing (and tucking into) their favourite.

1. Beat the butter, sugar and icing sugar in a stand mixer fitted with the beater, on medium speed for 3–5 minutes, until pale and creamy, scraping down the sides of the bowl from time to time.

2. Add the egg yolks and vanilla and beat until thoroughly combined. Add the flour and salt and mix until the dough comes together into a smooth ball. Be careful not to overwork the dough or the biscuits could end up tough, rather than crisp and crumbly.

3. Shape the dough into 2 neat sausage shapes, each about 5cm in diameter. Cover and chill for 1–2 hours, until firm.

4. Meanwhile, make the crumble topping. Tip the flour into a bowl and rub in the cubed butter with your fingertips until only small flecks remain. Add both sugars and mix using your fingertips until the crumble starts to clump together. Cover and chill until needed.

5. Heat the oven to 180°C/160°C fan/Gas 4.

6. Cut the chilled dough into twenty-four 1cm-thick slices and press each evenly into the base of a muffin hollow. Sprinkle the crumble mixture around the edge of each biscuit, leaving a space in the middle. Spoon ½–1 teaspoon of jam, lemon curd or chocolate hazelnut spread into the space, or fill it with a chocolate button (or make six biscuits of each filling).

7. Bake the biscuits for about 18 minutes, until the crumble is golden and the filling is bubbling or melted. Leave to cool in the trays for 5–10 minutes, then carefully remove using a palette knife and transfer to a wire rack to cool completely.

Photography overleaf

300ml just-boiled water
1 tea bag (breakfast tea)
125g sultanas
125g raisins
200g dark brown soft sugar
75g unsalted butter, cubed,
    plus extra for greasing
300g self-raising flour
pinch of salt
2 eggs
2 tbsp malt extract
salted butter, to serve
    (optional)

YOU WILL NEED
450g loaf tins x 2, greased,
    then lined (base and
    sides) with baking paper

Makes
2 loaves

Hands on
20 mins

plus soaking

Bake
40 mins

Malt Loaf

Sliced and spread with butter, malt loaf is the perfect teatime snack, or a treat tucked into a lunch or picnic box. It's an easy bake for children to try – once the fruit has soaked (start this the day before you intend to bake), you simply mix everything together, spoon it into the tin and pop it in the oven.

1. Pour the just-boiled water into a mixing bowl, add the tea bag, stir, and leave to infuse for 4 minutes. Add the sultanas, raisins and sugar, then stir to dissolve the sugar. Leave to cool for about 30 minutes.

2. Squeeze the tea bag to extract as much flavour as possible and discard. Cover the bowl and leave the dried fruit at room temperature for at least 4 hours, but preferably overnight, to absorb some of the tea and become plump and juicy.

3. Heat the oven to 180°C/160°C fan/Gas 4.

4. Melt the butter either in the microwave or a small saucepan over a low heat.

5. Sift the flour and salt into a large mixing bowl and make a well in the centre. Add the melted butter, eggs and malt extract and whisk gently to break up the eggs. Add the dried fruit and tea mixture (including the soaking liquid) and mix until smooth and combined.

6. Divide the mixture equally between the lined tins. Bake on the middle shelf for about 40 minutes, until the loaves are browned, well risen and a skewer inserted into the centres comes out clean. Leave to cool in the tins on a wire rack for 5 minutes, then carefully turn out and leave to cool completely.

7. Wrap the cooled loaves or place them in an airtight box or tin and set aside – for 24 hours, ideally, to allow the flavour to develop. When you're ready to serve, slice the loaves, and spread the slices with salted butter, if you wish.

CHAPTER THREE

Celebrate

Recipes

CHERRY AND CHOCOLATE BAKED ALASKA

FRUIT AND FLOWERS WEDDING CAKE

ICED AND SPICED BISCUITS

PESTO STAR BREAD

LAURA'S CHOCOLATE AND SALTED CARAMEL CAKE

NOVELTY FROG CAKE

RHUBARB, ROSE AND PISTACHIO LAYER CAKE

DUIVEKATER

STRAWBERRY AND ELDERFLOWER CAKE

SPRITZ COOKIES

PRUE'S MILLE CRÊPE CAKE

HUMMINGBIRD CAKE

CHRISTMAS LOG CAKE

FOR THE PARFAIT
8 egg yolks
150g caster sugar
1 tsp vanilla paste
175g 70% dark chocolate,
    roughly chopped
600ml double cream

FOR THE CHERRY COMPOTE
250g frozen or canned
    pitted cherries
50g caster sugar
1 tsp vanilla paste

FOR THE CAKE BASE
2 eggs
50g caster sugar
40g plain flour
20g cocoa powder

FOR THE MERINGUE
5 egg whites, at room
    temperature
pinch of salt
225g caster sugar

YOU WILL NEED
1.75-litre pudding basin,
    inside brushed with oil
    and lined with cling film
300ml pudding basin,
    wrapped in cling film
20cm cake tin, greased,
    then base-lined with
    baking paper
large ovenproof serving
    plate; or baking sheet,
    greased, then lined

Serves
8–10

Hands on
1½ hours

Bake
15 mins

plus freezing

Cherry and Chocolate Baked Alaska

Parfait, ice-cream, cherry compote and fluffy meringue – topped with sparklers, if you wish – whether it's a New Year or a new job you're celebrating, this decadent twist on a classic baked Alaska is the ultimate party piece to bring to the table.

1. Make the parfait. Tip the egg yolks into a heatproof bowl. Tip the sugar into a small saucepan, add 4 tablespoons of water and place over a low heat, stirring occasionally to dissolve the sugar. Bring to the boil and cook on a high heat for about 1 minute, until syrupy. Pour the hot syrup over the egg yolks, whisking continuously until smooth.

2. Set the bowl over a pan of simmering water. Add the vanilla paste and whisk for about 3 minutes, until doubled in volume, thick and mousse-like, and the mixture leaves a ribbon trail when you lift the whisk. Remove from the heat and plunge the bottom of the bowl into a sink of cold water to stop the cooking process. Leave to cool to room temperature.

3. Meanwhile, melt the chocolate in a heatproof bowl set over a pan of barely simmering water, or in the microwave on a low setting. Stir until smooth, then remove from the heat and leave to cool slightly.

4. In a separate bowl, whip the cream to soft peaks.

5. Weigh the egg mixture and divide it equally between 2 bowls, then cover and chill one of them. Add the melted chocolate to the unchilled bowl and mix until smooth. Fold in half the whipped cream until no streaks remain. Cover and chill the remaining cream.

6. Spoon the chocolate parfait mixture into the lined pudding basin and press the smaller, wrapped bowl into the middle to make a parfait shell. Cover and freeze for 2 hours, until firm.

Continues overleaf

7. Meanwhile, make the cherry compote. Combine the cherries, sugar and vanilla paste in a small pan over a low–medium heat, stirring until the sugar dissolves. Cook the cherries, allowing them to bubble gently for 20 minutes, until jammy. Cool, then cover until needed.

8. Make the cake base. Whisk the eggs and sugar in the bowl of a stand mixer fitted with the whisk, on medium speed for 3 minutes, until combined. Increase the speed and whisk until tripled in volume, thick and mousse-like, and the mixture leaves a ribbon trail when you lift the whisk. Heat the oven to 180°C/160°C fan/Gas 4.

9. Sift the flour and cocoa powder into the bowl and, using a large metal spoon or a spatula, fold in. Spoon the mixture into the lined cake tin and level out. Bake for 10 minutes, until risen and firm to the touch. Remove from the oven and turn out onto a wire rack to cool.

10. Meanwhile, make the vanilla ice-cream layer. Fold the reserved whipped cream into the remaining egg-yolk mixture. Remove the pudding basin containing the parfait from the freezer and carefully remove the smaller bowl. Spoon half the cherry compote into the hollow, then spoon the vanilla ice cream on top. Cover and return to the freezer for at least 6 hours, but preferably overnight, until frozen.

11. Just before serving, heat the oven to 220°C/200°C fan/Gas 7.

12. Make the meringue. Whisk the egg whites with the pinch of salt in the bowl of a stand mixer fitted with the whisk until they form soft peaks. Add the caster sugar, 2 tablespoons at a time, whisking well between each addition. Whisk on high speed for a further 2 minutes, until the sugar has completely dissolved and the meringue is smooth, very stiff and glossy.

13. Remove the bowl containing the parfait/ice cream from the freezer. Place the chocolate cake on the large ovenproof serving plate or lined baking sheet and spoon the reserved cherry compote into the middle.

14. Working quickly, turn the parfait/ice cream out of the bowl onto the cake base and peel off the cling film. Spoon the meringue evenly all over the ice cream until completely covered, then, using a palette knife, make swirls in the meringue.

15. Again working quickly, place the Alaska in the oven on the lower-middle shelf. Bake for 3–4 minutes, until the outside of the meringue is crisp, golden and starting to caramelise at the edges. Serve immediately (with sparklers, of course!).

FOR THE LEMON CURD
juice and finely grated zest
    of 1½ unwaxed lemons
1 egg
2 egg yolks (save the
    whites for the meringue
    buttercream)
75g caster sugar
40g unsalted butter,
    softened
pinch of salt

FOR THE CARROT CAKE
(DOUBLE THIS RECIPE)
275g coarsely grated carrots
    (grated weight)
75g pecans, toasted
    and chopped
50g desiccated coconut
50g raisins or sultanas
juice and finely grated zest
    of ½ unwaxed orange
3 eggs
250ml sunflower oil
275g caster sugar
2 tbsp whole milk
2 tsp vanilla paste
250g plain flour
1½ tsp baking powder
½ tsp bicarbonate of soda
1 tsp ground cinnamon
pinch of salt

FOR THE LEMON SPONGE
225g unsalted butter,
    softened
225g caster sugar
4 eggs, lightly beaten
225g self-raising flour
1 tsp baking powder
pinch of salt
finely grated zest of
    1 unwaxed lemon
juice of ½ lemon
2 tbsp whole milk

Continues overleaf

*Serves
60*

*Hands on
4 hours*

*Bake
2 hours*

plus chilling

Fruit and Flowers Wedding Cake

There are two types of sponge in this dreamy wedding cake: carrot filled with cream-cheese frosting, and lemon filled with buttercream and lemon curd, so something for everyone. You can prepare and refrigerate the lemon curd up to five days ahead of the big day, and the cakes, cream-cheese frosting and meringue buttercream a day ahead. You could even make and freeze the cakes well in advance, then defrost them in time to construct the cake on the day itself. The results are beautiful – made at home it may be, but this wedding cake is more than worthy of any once-in-a-lifetime day.

1. Make the lemon curd. Place the lemon juice and zest in a heatproof glass or ceramic bowl. Add the whole egg and yolks and whisk to combine. Add the sugar, butter and salt, then mix well.

2. Set the bowl over a pan of simmering water and stir frequently to melt the butter and dissolve the sugar. Continue cooking for about 10 minutes, stirring frequently, until the curd thickens enough to coat the back of a spoon, and leaves a ribbon trail when you lift the spoon.

3. Remove from the heat and pass the curd through a fine sieve into a bowl or large jar. Leave to cool, then cover and chill for up to 5 days.

4. Heat the oven to 180°C/160°C fan/Gas 4.

5. Make the carrot cake (double this recipe to make two cakes). Mix together the carrots, pecans, coconut, raisins or sultanas, orange juice and zest in a large mixing bowl.

6. In a separate large bowl, using an electric hand whisk, beat the eggs, sunflower oil, sugar, milk and vanilla for 3–4 minutes, until light and airy. Fold in the carrot mixture.

Continues overleaf

**FOR THE MERINGUE
BUTTERCREAM
(DOUBLE THIS RECIPE)**
275g caster sugar
4 egg whites
pinch of salt
350g unsalted butter,
    softened
2 tsp vanilla paste

**FOR THE CREAM-CHEESE
FROSTING**
100g unsalted butter,
    softened
4 tbsp runny honey
2 tsp vanilla paste
400g full-fat cream cheese

TO DECORATE
edible fresh flowers
    (choose colours to
    match your theme)
berries (optional)

YOU WILL NEED
25cm cake tin (8cm deep),
    greased, then base-lined
    with baking paper
    (used twice)
18cm sandwich tins x 3,
    greased, then base-lined
    with baking paper
1 large piping bag fitted
    with a large plain nozzle
20cm cake board
1cm ribbon nozzle
cake-decorating turntable
6 cake dowels

7. Sift together the flour, baking powder, bicarbonate of soda, cinnamon and salt into the bowl and mix well, using a large spoon or rubber spatula, until thoroughly combined.

8. Carefully pour the mixture into the lined 25cm tin and level with a palette knife. Bake on the middle shelf for about 45 minutes, or until a skewer inserted into the centre comes out clean. Leave to cool in the tin for 10 minutes, then turn out onto a wire rack. Turn the cake the right way up and leave to cool completely.

9. Grease and line the cake tin again and prepare and bake the second carrot cake, following the same method.

10. Make the lemon sponge. Beat the butter and sugar in a stand mixer fitted with the beater, on medium speed for 3–5 minutes, until pale and creamy, scraping down the sides of the bowl from time to time.

11. Add the eggs, a little at a time, beating well between each addition. Sift the flour, baking powder and salt into the bowl and mix until just combined. Add the lemon zest, lemon juice and milk and beat again until smooth.

12. Divide the mixture equally between the lined 18cm tins and level with a palette knife. Bake on the middle shelves for 15 minutes, until risen, golden brown and a skewer inserted into the centres comes out clean. Leave to cool in the tins for 3 minutes, then turn out onto a wire rack to cool completely.

13. Make the meringue buttercream (double this recipe). Put the sugar, egg whites and salt into a medium, heatproof bowl set over a pan of simmering water. Add 2 tablespoons of water and whisk until the sugar completely dissolves and the mixture becomes foamy. Continue for about 3 minutes, whisking continuously, until the mixture thickens and increases in volume, turns from opaque to bright white, and leaves a ribbon trail when you lift the whisk.

14. Pour the mixture into the bowl of a stand mixer fitted with the whisk and beat on medium–high speed for 3–4 minutes, until the mixture doubles in volume and is thick, stiff, glossy and cold to the touch.

15. Gradually, add the softened butter to the cooled meringue mixture, beating continuously until smooth. Add the vanilla and mix again to combine. Spoon into a clean bowl and cover until ready to use.

Continues overleaf

16. Make the second batch of meringue buttercream, following the same method. Then, use the buttercream to half fill the piping bag fitted with the plain nozzle (keep topping up as necessary).

17. Assemble the lemon cake. Place one lemon sponge on the 20cm cake board and pipe a ring of buttercream around the top outside edge. Spoon half the lemon curd into the middle of the ring. Top with the second lemon sponge and repeat with the buttercream and the remaining lemon curd. Top with the third lemon sponge.

18. Create a crumb coat: spread the top and sides of the cake with a thin, even layer of buttercream, then chill for 30 minutes.

19. Fit the piping bag with the ribbon nozzle and top it up with buttercream as necessary. Place the lemon cake on the cake-decorating turntable. Starting at the bottom of the cake, pipe neat buttercream ribbons around the cake to cover the sides, gently spinning the turntable as you pipe. Continue piping ribbons to cover the top of the cake. Chill until ready to assemble.

20. Make the cream-cheese frosting for the carrot cake. With an electric hand whisk, or a stand mixer fitted with the beater, beat the butter until pale and soft. Add the honey and vanilla and mix again. Add the cream cheese and mix gently until smooth.

21. Using a long, serrated bread knife, cut each carrot cake in half horizontally. Place 1 sponge on a serving plate and spread with one third of the cream-cheese frosting. Sandwich with a second sponge and spread with another third of the frosting. Top with a third sponge and the final third of frosting. Finish with the final sponge. Cover the top and sides of the carrot cake with a thin layer of buttercream to form a crumb coat, then cover the buttercream and set aside. Chill the cake for 30 minutes.

22. Spread the remaining buttercream evenly over the top and sides of the carrot cake and chill again for 1 hour, until firm or ready to serve.

23. To assemble, measure and cut the cake dowels to the same height as the assembled carrot cake and push 4–6 rods into the middle of the cake, in a well-spaced triangle formation. Carefully lift the lemon cake on the cake board on top of the rods, making sure it is supported.

24. Decorate the cake with fresh flowers, and with berries, too, if you wish.

2 tbsp golden syrup
1 large egg yolk
200g plain flour,
    plus extra for dusting
½ tsp baking powder
1 tsp ground ginger
1 tsp ground cinnamon
¼ tsp ground cardamom
¼ tsp freshly grated nutmeg
pinch of salt
¼ tsp freshly ground
    black pepper
100g unsalted butter,
    cubed and chilled
75g light muscovado sugar

FOR THE ICING
500g icing sugar
2 egg whites
assorted food-colouring
    pastes

YOU WILL NEED
teardrop- or paisley-shaped
    cutters in assorted sizes
2 baking sheets,
    greased, then lined
    with baking paper
small piping bags and
    small writing nozzles

Makes about 25

Hands on 2 hours plus chilling

Bake 12 mins

Iced and Spiced Biscuits

Diwali, the Hindu festival of lights, is the inspiration for these gorgeous biscuits, decorated in bright colours with dainty, paisley patterns. Add edible silver balls and glitter to finish the biscuits with their own sparkle, too.

1. Beat together the golden syrup and egg yolk in a small bowl, then set aside.

2. Sift the flour, baking powder, spices, salt and black pepper into the bowl of a food processor and pulse to combine. Add the butter and pulse again for 1 minute. Add the sugar and pulse again to combine.

3. With the motor running, add the egg-yolk mixture, then pulse again until the mixture starts to clump. Turn the mixture out of the bowl and knead into a ball. Flatten into a disc, cover and chill for about 2 hours, until firm.

4. On a lightly floured work surface, roll out the dough until 2–3mm thick. Using the cutters, stamp out teardrop or paisley shapes in assorted sizes and arrange on the lined baking sheets. Re-roll the trimmings and stamp out more shapes until you have used up all the dough. Chill the biscuits for 20 minutes.

5. Meanwhile, heat the oven to 170°C/150°C fan/Gas 3.

6. Bake the biscuits for 10–12 minutes, until firm and lightly browned at the edges. Leave to cool on the baking sheets.

7. Make the icing. Sift the icing sugar into the bowl of a stand mixer fitted with the whisk. Add the egg whites and 2 tablespoons of water and whisk for about 2 minutes, until smooth and thick.

8. Divide the icing between 5 bowls and tint each one a different colour – the colours can become more vivid with time, so add a tiny amount of paste at a time.

Continues overleaf

9. For the first stage of decorating the biscuits the icing needs to be thick enough to hold a firm ribbon trail – add a drop more water if needed. Start with one colour and spoon half the icing into a piping bag fitted with a writing nozzle, twist the top to seal. Pipe a continuous line around the edge of some of the biscuits.

10. Repeat with the other colours until all the biscuits have a piped outline. Leave to set for 30 minutes, storing the filled piping bags in an airtight container and covering the bowls of remaining icing to prevent it from drying out.

11. Starting with 1 bowl of the coloured icing, add a drop more water and mix to loosen to a flooding consistency. Spoon ½–1 teaspoon of icing, the same colour as the outline, onto each biscuit. Using a teaspoon or small palette knife, tease the icing into the shape to fill smoothly. Repeat to fill all the outlines. Leave the iced biscuits to dry and harden for about 4 hours.

12. Using contrasting colours, pipe paisley patterns, dots, flowers, stars and lines over each biscuit, and leave to set for another 2 hours before serving.

500g strong white
   bread flour
7g fast-action dried yeast
1 tsp caster sugar
½ tsp salt
275ml whole milk,
   plus 1 tbsp to glaze
50g unsalted butter,
   softened
1 egg, lightly beaten
150g homemade, or
   good-quality shop-
   bought basil pesto
3 rounded tbsp finely grated
   Parmesan cheese
freshly ground black pepper
crushed sea salt, for
   sprinkling (optional)

YOU WILL NEED
large baking sheet,
   greased, then lined
   with baking paper
glass with a 6–7cm-
   diameter rim
large proving bag (optional)

Serves
10–12

Hands on
45 mins

Bake
30 mins

plus rising

Pesto Star Bread

*This savoury Christmas star bread – tear and share at its best –
is flavoured with pesto and Parmesan. It looks stunning in the
middle of a festive table, but is equally enticing as the centrepiece
of a celebratory buffet at any other time of year. You can use
sun-dried tomato pesto, if you prefer.*

1. Tip the flour into the bowl of a stand mixer fitted with the dough
hook. Add the yeast, sugar and salt, then season well with pepper
and mix well to combine.

2. Gently warm the milk either in a small pan over a low heat or in a
microwave. Add it to the mixing bowl with the butter and egg. Mix on
a low speed until combined, then knead on medium speed for another
3–4 minutes, until smooth and elastic. Shape the dough into a ball,
then return it to the bowl, cover and leave to rise for 45 minutes to
1 hour, until doubled in size.

3. Turn out the dough and knead gently for 30 seconds to knock
out any large air pockets. Weigh and divide the dough into 4 equal
pieces. Shape each piece into a neat ball, cover loosely and leave to
rest on the work surface for 5 minutes to allow the gluten to relax.

4. Lightly flour your work surface and roll out 1 piece of dough to
a neat 28cm disc, using a dinner plate as a guide. Then, carefully
transfer the disc to the lined baking sheet. Roll out the remaining
3 pieces to the same size.

5. Spread 50g of the pesto over the first dough disc, leaving a
2cm border around the edge. Scatter with 1 rounded tablespoon
of the Parmesan and lightly brush the border with milk. Carefully
and neatly top with the second dough disc, then spread with another
50g of pesto and 1 rounded tablespoon of Parmesan. Repeat this
layering, finishing with the fourth disc of dough.

Continues overleaf

6. Place the glass with the 6–7cm rim in the middle of the dough. Using a long-bladed knife, cut the dough into 16 evenly spaced strips, from the edge of the glass to the outside edge of the dough.

7. Pick up two adjacent strips. Holding one in each hand, twist the strip in your right hand twice clockwise and the strip in your left hand twice anticlockwise, so that you are twisting them in opposite directions to each other. Then, twist, press and pinch the ends together to seal into a point.

8. Repeat all the way round the dough until you have an eight-pointed star. Remove the glass.

9. Loosely cover the dough (or place the baking tray in a proving bag) and leave to prove for 30–45 minutes.

10. Heat the oven to 190°C/170°C fan/Gas 5.

11. Lightly brush the bread with milk. Bake for about 30 minutes, until golden brown and well risen. Leave to cool to room temperature before serving sprinkled with crushed salt, if you wish.

Serves
16

Hands on
1½ hours
plus chilling

Bake
25 mins

BAKER'S FAVOURITE

Laura's Chocolate and Salted Caramel Cake

This indulgent cake combines two of my favourite flavours: rich, fudgy chocolate and salted caramel. I'm always asked to make it for family members' birthdays – it's a proper celebration piece, a showstopper to be met with guaranteed 'oohs' and 'aahs'.

FOR THE SPONGE
95g cocoa powder, sifted
240g light brown soft sugar
2½ tsp vanilla paste
175ml just-boiled water
420g plain flour
1 tsp baking powder
1 tsp bicarbonate of soda
250g salted butter, softened
280g caster sugar
4 large eggs

FOR THE SALTED CARAMEL
150g caster sugar
150ml double cream
1 tsp vanilla extract
1 tsp sea salt

FOR THE BUTTERCREAM
220g egg whites
    (about 6 large whites)
320g caster sugar
470g unsalted butter,
    cubed and softened
4 tsp vanilla extract

TO DECORATE
caramel chocolates,
    popcorn or honeycomb

YOU WILL NEED
20cm sandwich tins x 4,
    greased, then base-lined
    with baking paper
25cm cake board
cake scraper
small paper piping bag
large piping bag fitted
    with a 2D nozzle or
    open star nozzle

1. Heat the oven to 180°C/160°C fan/Gas 4.

2. Make the sponge. Whisk the cocoa powder, light brown soft sugar, vanilla paste and just-boiled water in a mixing bowl until smooth. Leave to cool for 5 minutes. Sift together the flour, baking powder and bicarbonate of soda in a separate bowl.

3. Beat the butter and caster sugar in a stand mixer fitted with the beater, on medium speed for 3–5 minutes, until pale and creamy, scraping down the sides of the bowl from time to time.

4. Beat in the eggs, one at a time, mixing in 1 tablespoon of the flour mixture after each egg. Fold in the remaining flour mixture, a third at a time, mixing well until incorporated, then fold in the cooled cocoa mixture.

5. Divide the sponge mixture equally between the lined tins and level with a palette knife. Bake on the middle shelf for 20–25 minutes, until risen and a skewer inserted into the centres comes out clean. Remove from the oven, leave to cool in the tins for 5 minutes, then turn out onto wire racks to cool completely.

6. Meanwhile, make the salted caramel. Put the caster sugar and 6 tablespoons of water in a medium saucepan over a medium heat. Cook for 6–8 minutes, without stirring, until the caramel starts to turn deep amber. Remove from the heat and place the pan in a bowl of cold water to stop the cooking process.

Continues overleaf

7. Slowly whisk the cream and vanilla extract into the caramel until you have a thick pouring consistency (if necessary return the pan to a low heat, stirring continuously, to reduce a little). Stir in the sea salt and leave to cool.

8. Make the buttercream. Whisk the egg whites and sugar together in a heatproof bowl until smooth. Set the bowl over a pan of simmering water and heat for about 5 minutes, whisking occasionally, until the sugar dissolves – the mixture should feel smooth, not grainy, between your fingertips.

9. Pour the egg-white mixture into the bowl of a stand mixer fitted with the whisk and whisk for about 7 minutes to stiff peaks. Add the butter, then whisk for about 5 minutes, until smooth and glossy. Don't panic if the mixture appears to curdle or turn lumpy – keep whisking until it becomes smooth. Add the vanilla extract and, 1 tablespoon at a time, add 5 tablespoons of the cooled caramel, until smooth.

10. Level the cakes if necessary and divide the buttercream between 3 bowls. Secure one of the sponges to the cake board using a little of one of the bowls of buttercream.

11. Using the buttercream from one of the bowls, spread it over the top of the sponge on the cake board, and on top of two other sponges, stacking them on top of one another. Top with the remaining sponge.

12. Using the buttercream from the second bowl, carefully spread it over the outside of the cake with a palette knife. For the semi-naked look, run a cake scraper around the outside of the cake with a firm pressure, so parts of the cake appear through the buttercream. Chill for 30 minutes.

13. Remove the cake from the fridge and pour the cooled salted caramel into the paper piping bag, twist the top to seal and snip the end. Pipe around and over the edge of the cake to create drips running down the side of the cake. Spread the remainder of the caramel over the top.

14. Spoon the final third of buttercream into the piping bag fitted with the nozzle and pipe around the top of the cake. Do not pipe too close to the edge as the buttercream can slide off. Decorate the cake with caramel chocolates, popcorn or honeycomb.

Serves
12-16

Hands on
1½ hours

Bake
30 mins

FOR THE SPONGE
350g unsalted butter, softened
350g caster sugar
2 tsp vanilla extract
6 eggs, lightly beaten
300g plain flour
50g cornflour
4 tsp baking powder
pinch of salt
5 tbsp whole milk, at room temperature

FOR THE BUTTERCREAM
200g unsalted butter, softened
400g icing sugar, sifted
2 tsp vanilla extract
2–3 tbsp whole milk, at room temperature

TO DECORATE
2 heaped tbsp raspberry or apricot jam
1kg ready-to-roll white fondant icing
green, red and black food-colouring pastes
icing sugar, for dusting
1 tube of black writing icing

YOU WILL NEED
1 muffin tin, lined with 2 paper cupcake cases
23cm sandwich tins x 2, greased, then base-lined with greased baking paper
4cm fluted cutter
2cm and 3cm round cutters

Novelty Frog Cake

The basic sponge and decorating ideas in this simple-to-make, fun, froggie birthday cake lend themselves to a whole herd of other animal faces, too. So if it's lions, cows, pigs or pandas your children love, just use different colour fondants to make the features.

1. Heat the oven to 180°C/160°C fan/Gas 4.

2. Make the sponge. Beat the butter and sugar in a stand mixer fitted with the beater, on medium speed for 3–5 minutes, until pale and creamy, scraping down the sides of the bowl from time to time. Add the vanilla extract and mix again.

3. Add the eggs, a little at a time, beating well between each addition.

4. Sift together the flour, cornflour, baking powder and salt into the bowl. Add the milk and beat, mixing slowly at first, until silky smooth, scraping down the sides of the bowl from time to time.

5. Half-fill the two cupcake cases with the mixture. Divide the remainder equally between the lined cake tins and level with a palette knife. Bake the large cakes on the middle shelves for about 30 minutes, until golden, well-risen and a skewer inserted into the centres comes out clean. At the same time, bake the cupcakes for about 12 minutes, until golden and well-risen.

6. Leave the large cakes to cool in the tins on a wire rack for 3–4 minutes, then turn out and leave to cool completely. Remove the cupcakes to the wire rack to cool, then remove the paper cases.

7. Meanwhile, make the buttercream. Beat the butter until pale and light, then gradually add the icing sugar, milk and vanilla extract, and continue beating until pale and fluffy.

8. Using a long, serrated sponge or bread knife, level the top of each large cake if necessary. Place one sponge on a serving plate and spread the top with the 2 heaped tablespoons of jam.

Continues overleaf

9. Spread the underside of the second sponge with 3 tablespoons of the buttercream and sandwich the cakes together. Cover the top and sides with an even, smooth layer of buttercream. Chill for 20 minutes while you prepare the fondant icing.

10. Separate out 150g of the white fondant, wrap and set aside. Using the green food-colouring paste, tint the remaining fondant, kneading well to an even colour. Cut off 100g of the green fondant, wrap and set aside.

11. Dust the work surface with icing sugar and roll out the large piece of green fondant to a neat disc, large enough to cover the top and sides of the cake. Using the rolling pin, carefully transfer the green fondant disc to the cake, covering it neatly and evenly. Using the palms of your hands, smooth the fondant over the top and sides and trim off any excess around the base.

12. Make the frog's eyes. Cut the reserved 100g of the green fondant in half, then roll each half into a 2mm-thick disc. Cover each cupcake neatly with green fondant, trimming off any excess. Slice a quarter off the side of each cupcake and position the larger pieces as eyes on top of the large cake, cut-sides down, with the top of each cupcake facing you.

13. Divide the reserved white fondant icing into thirds and, using the colouring pastes, colour one third black and another third red, leaving the remaining fondant white.

14. Dust the work surface with icing sugar, roll out the white icing to 2mm thick. Using the 4cm fluted cutter, stamp out two 3–4cm discs. Roll out the black icing until 2mm thick and stamp out two 2cm discs. Slice a small section off each disc (black and white) to give a flat edge. Very lightly brush the white discs with water and stick them onto the front of the green-iced cupcakes, lining up the flat edges, to make the whites of the eyes. Brush the black fondant discs with water and position in the centre of the white fondant pieces, again lining up the flat edges, to make pupils.

15. Roll out the red icing until 2mm thick, and stamp out two 2–3cm discs. Lightly brush these with water and stick them to the top of the cake to make the cheeks. Using the black writing icing, pipe a smile and nostrils on top of the cake. Add little flies around the sides, if you wish. Once the cake is decorated, leave the icing to set at room temperature or in the fridge for 1 hour before serving.

FOR THE SPONGE
100g ground almonds
40g ground pistachios
120g gluten-free self-
raising flour, sifted
225g unsalted butter,
softened
225g golden caster sugar
4 eggs
50ml soured cream
1 tsp vanilla paste
pinch of salt
250g rhubarb, washed,
trimmed and cut into
1cm dice

FOR THE RHUBARB
& ROSE COMPOTE
200g rhubarb, trimmed
and cut into 2–3cm pieces
50g caster sugar
3–5 drops rose water

FOR THE VANILLA
ROSE SYRUP
50g caster sugar
½ tsp vanilla paste
2–3 drops rose water

FOR THE VANILLA
BUTTERCREAM
225g unsalted butter,
softened
420g icing sugar, sifted
1 tsp vanilla paste
3 tbsp whole milk

TO DECORATE
edible flowers (such as
roses and abutilons)
dried edible rose petals
6 lemon balm or mint sprigs
5 pistachio kernels,
finely chopped

YOU WILL NEED
15cm sandwich tins x 3,
greased, then base-lined
with baking paper
1 medium piping bag fitted
with a large plain nozzle
15cm cake board
cake scraper

Serves
12-16

Hands on
1½ hours

Bake
35 mins

Rhubarb, Rose and Pistachio Layer Cake

Middle Eastern and British flavours work together in this deliciously nutty layer cake. The richness of the almonds, pistachios and fragrant rose is offset by the tangy, tart rhubarb. It makes a gorgeous summer celebration cake.

1. Heat the oven to 180°C/160°C fan/Gas 4.

2. Make the sponge. Stir the ground almonds, pistachios and gluten-free flour together in a mixing bowl.

3. Beat the butter and sugar in a stand mixer fitted with the beater, on medium speed for 7–10 minutes, until pale and creamy, scraping down the sides of the bowl from time to time.

4. Add the eggs, one at a time, beating well between each addition. If the mixture starts to curdle, add a spoonful of the flour mixture. Beat in the soured cream.

5. Fold in the flour mixture, vanilla and salt, and the diced rhubarb.

6. Divide the mixture equally between the lined sandwich tins and level with a palette knife. Bake on the middle shelves for 30–35 minutes, until risen and golden, and a skewer inserted into the centres comes out clean. Leave to cool in the tins on a wire rack.

7. Meanwhile, make the compote. Mix the rhubarb pieces and sugar in a pan and leave to stand for about 10 minutes while the rhubarb releases some liquid. Bring to the boil, then reduce the heat and simmer for about 5 minutes, stirring occasionally, until softened. Remove from the heat and add the rose water to taste, then leave to cool.

Continues overleaf

8. Make the vanilla rose syrup. Pour 50ml water into a small pan, add the sugar, vanilla paste and the rose water to taste, then stir over a low heat until the sugar dissolves and it becomes syrupy. Leave to cool.

9. Prick holes over the warm sponges with a cocktail stick, then brush over the vanilla rose syrup. Leave to cool completely in the tins.

10. Make the vanilla buttercream. Beat the butter in a stand mixer fitted with the beater, on slow speed for 5 minutes, until pale and creamy. Add the icing sugar, a little at a time, then add the vanilla paste and milk and beat to a smooth, fluffy buttercream. Spoon into the piping bag fitted with a plain nozzle and twist the end to seal.

11. Pipe dots of buttercream onto the cake board. Place one of the sponges on the board and pipe buttercream on top, spreading it evenly to the edges. Pipe a ring of buttercream around the edge of the sponge and fill the middle with the rhubarb compote. Place a second sponge on top and repeat.

12. Add the final sponge and pipe a generous layer of buttercream on top. Smooth it out, or make a swirl pattern in the buttercream with a large offset palette knife, if you wish.

13. Pipe thick stripes of buttercream around the side of the cake and scrape away the excess with a cake scraper to give a semi-naked finish, with patches of sponge peeping through.

14. Decorate with fresh edible flowers, dried rose petals, lemon balm or mint sprigs and chopped pistachios.

225ml whole milk
450g strong white
    bread flour
7g fast-action dried yeast
75g caster sugar
½ tsp salt
¼ tsp grated nutmeg
¼ tsp ground cardamom
¼ tsp ground cinnamon
finely grated zest of
    ½ unwaxed lemon
75g unsalted butter,
    softened
1 egg, beaten, plus
    another for brushing

YOU WILL NEED
large baking sheet,
    greased, then lined
    with baking paper

Serves
8

Hands on
30 mins

Bake
30 mins

plus rising

Duivekater

This unusual loaf is shaped to resemble a shin bone – a nod to its northern Dutch origins as an offering (in lieu of an animal sacrifice) to protect against the Devil. It is flavoured with lemon and spices and was traditionally given as a gift at Christmas. The name is said to derive from 'Devil's tomcat'.

1. Gently warm the milk either in a small pan over a low heat or in the microwave.

2. Tip the flour into the bowl of a stand mixer fitted with the dough hook. Add the yeast, sugar, salt, nutmeg, cardamom and cinnamon and stir to combine. Make a well in the centre and add the lemon zest, warm milk, butter and egg. Mix on medium speed until combined, then mix for another 5 minutes, until the dough is smooth and elastic.

3. Turn out the dough onto a work surface, knead briefly by hand and shape into a ball. Return to the bowl, cover, and leave to rise for about 1 hour, until the dough is light and bouncy and has doubled in size.

4. Turn out the dough onto a lightly floured work surface and knead for 30 seconds to knock out any large air pockets. Cover with an upturned bowl and leave to rest for 5–10 minutes.

5. Roll out the dough into an oval shape, about 40cm long and 3cm thick, and transfer to the lined baking sheet. Using a sharp knife, at each end make a 10cm-long cut down the middle. Slightly stretch out the ends and twist them inwards into coils. Cover loosely with a clean tea towel and leave to prove for 1 hour, or until the dough has risen and become light and puffy.

6. Heat the oven to 190°C/170°C fan/Gas 5. Brush the loaf with the egg and, using a sharp knife, cut decorative patterns into the top. Bake on the middle shelf for 10 minutes, then reduce the heat to 180°C/160°C fan/Gas 4 and bake for another 20 minutes, or until the bread is well risen, golden brown and the underside sounds hollow then tapped. Leave to cool on a wire rack before slicing.

FOR THE SPONGE
250g unsalted butter,
   softened
275g caster sugar
5 eggs
2 tbsp elderflower cordial
2 tbsp whole milk
1 tsp vanilla extract
   or paste
finely grated zest of
   ½ unwaxed lemon
275g gluten-free
   self-raising flour
1 tsp gluten-free
   baking powder
¼ tsp xanthan gum
pinch of salt

FOR THE MERINGUE
2 egg whites
pinch of salt
100g caster sugar

FOR THE FILLING
300g strawberries,
   hulled and sliced
4 tbsp elderflower cordial
300ml double cream
4 rounded tbsp homemade
   or good-quality
   strawberry jam

TO DECORATE (OPTIONAL)
fresh elderflowers
handful of whole
   strawberries
icing sugar, for dusting

YOU WILL NEED
20cm sandwich tins x 3,
   greased, then base-lined
   with baking paper

Serves
10-12

Hands on
40 mins

Bake
30 mins

plus macerating

Strawberry and Elderflower Cake

This is just the cake for an early summer birthday, when the first sweet strawberries are in season and the elderflower blossom is still in the hedgerows. If you can't find elderflowers, scatter with edible rose petals instead. This cake's crowning glory, though, is the layer of meringue on top.

1. Heat the oven to 170°C/150°C fan/Gas 3.

2. Make the sponge. Beat the butter and sugar in a stand mixer fitted with the beater, on medium speed for 3–5 minutes, until pale and creamy, scraping down the sides of the bowl from time to time.

3. Add the eggs, one at a time, beating well between each addition. Add the elderflower cordial, milk, vanilla and lemon zest.

4. Sift together the flour, baking powder, xanthan gum and salt into the bowl and, using a rubber spatula, mix until roughly combined, then beat on medium speed for 30 seconds, until smooth. Divide the mixture equally between the lined tins and level with a palette knife.

5. Make the meringue. Whisk the egg whites and salt in a clean bowl to soft peaks. Add the sugar, 1 tablespoon at a time, whisking well between each addition until the meringue is smooth, stiff and glossy. Spoon the meringue over the top of one of the sponges, swirling to cover.

6. Bake the sponges on the middle shelf for about 25 minutes, until well risen, golden brown and a wooden skewer inserted into the centres comes out clean. Remove the two plain sponges from the oven, leaving the meringue-topped sponge to bake for another 5 minutes, then remove that from the oven, too.

Continues overleaf

7. Leave the plain sponges to cool in the tins for 2–3 minutes, then carefully turn them out onto a wire rack, remove the baking paper and leave to cool completely. Carefully remove the meringue-topped sponge from the tin, peel off the baking paper and leave to cool, meringue-side up.

8. Meanwhile, tip the strawberries for the filling into a bowl and mix in 1 tablespoon of the elderflower cordial, cover and leave to macerate for 30 minutes. Whip the double cream with the remaining 3 tablespoons of elderflower cordial to soft peaks.

9. Place one plain sponge on a serving plate and spread with half the strawberry jam. Cover the jam with half the whipped cream and arrange half the sliced strawberries on top.

10. Cover with the second plain sponge and repeat the layering of jam, cream and strawberries. Finally, place the meringue sponge on top and gently press the sponge layers together. Decorate with the fresh elderflowers and/or whole strawberries (if using), then dust with icing sugar, if you wish, and serve.

225g unsalted butter, softened
100g icing sugar, sifted
1 teaspoon vanilla extract
1 egg
250g plain flour
30g cornflour
20g ground almonds
pinch of salt
5–6 tsp apricot or strawberry jam (optional)
100g 70% dark chocolate, roughly chopped
chocolate vermicelli or sprinkles (optional)

YOU WILL NEED
large piping bag fitted with a medium star nozzle
2 baking sheets, greased, then lined with baking paper

Makes
18

Hands on
20 mins
plus chilling

Bake
17 mins

Spritz Cookies

These crisp, buttery biscuits are a German Christmas cookie traditionally made using a biscuit press – but a piping bag with a star-shaped nozzle makes the perfect alternative. It's also perhaps more fitting, given that the German word spritzen *means 'to squirt'!*

1. Beat the butter in a stand mixer fitted with the beater, on medium speed for 2–3 minutes, until really pale and soft. Reduce the speed to low, add the icing sugar and vanilla extract and combine. Return to medium speed and beat for another 2 minutes, until smooth. Add the egg and mix again to thoroughly combine.

2. Sift the flour and cornflour into the bowl, add the ground almonds and salt and mix again until smooth.

3. Spoon the mixture into the piping bag and twist the end to seal. Pipe rings, S-shapes or fingers onto the lined baking sheets, leaving a little space between each to allow for them to spread during baking. Chill for 30 minutes.

4. Heat the oven to 180°C/160°C fan/Gas 4.

5. Bake the biscuits for 16–17 minutes, until golden. Leave to cool on the baking sheets for 5 minutes, then transfer to a wire rack. Fill half the biscuits with ½ heaped teaspoon of jam, if using, then leave to cool. Leave the remainder to cool completely, just as they are.

6. Melt the chocolate in a heatproof bowl set over a pan of barely simmering water. Stir until smooth and remove from the heat. Leave to cool for 1 minute.

7. Dip one half each of the remaining biscuits into the melted chocolate (or all of them if you're not using jam). Scrape and shake off any excess, then scatter with vermicelli or sprinkles, if using. Transfer to a sheet of baking paper and leave to set for 30 minutes, then serve.

Photography overleaf

FOR THE BATTER

400ml whole milk
45g caster sugar
3 large eggs
25g unsalted butter, melted
125g plain flour
15g cornflour
½ tsp baking powder
15g matcha powder,
     plus extra for dusting
sunflower oil, for cooking

FOR THE WHITE CHOCOLATE FILLING

150g white chocolate
75ml double cream
2 large egg whites
70g caster sugar
1 tsp vanilla paste
½ tsp fine salt
225g unsalted butter,
     softened
400g strawberries, hulled

TO DECORATE

sliced strawberries
fresh mango, cut into
     5mm dice
freeze-dried raspberry
     pieces
desiccated coconut
edible flowers (white
     and purple are pretty)

YOU WILL NEED

sugar thermometer
mandoline or very
     sharp knife
30cm crêpe or frying pan
24cm crêpe or frying pan
20cm plate or cake-tin base
23cm shallow bowl, lined
     with cling film, leaving
     a 20cm overhang

Serves
10

Hands on
1 hour 20 mins

Cook
40 mins

plus chilling

JUDGE'S RECIPE

Prue's Mille Crêpe Cake

The crêpes in this beautiful, celebration centrepiece are made using matcha powder – finely ground green tea leaves that give a gorgeous, vivid colour. In Prue's recipe, they are layered with creamy, white chocolate and strawberry filling.

1. Make the batter. Gently heat the milk and sugar over a low heat for 2–3 minutes, stirring, until the sugar dissolves and the milk is warm.

2. Beat the eggs in a mixing bowl. Using a balloon whisk, slowly add the warm milk mixture to the eggs, whisking continuously. Add the melted butter and mix until combined.

3. Sift together the flour, cornflour, baking powder and matcha powder over the egg mixture and whisk until completely smooth. Pass through a sieve into a clean jug, then cover and chill for 30 minutes.

4. Meanwhile, make a white chocolate ganache for the filling. Melt the white chocolate with the cream in a heatproof bowl set over a pan of barely simmering water. Stir until smooth and remove from the heat, then leave to cool to room temperature.

5. Place the egg whites and sugar in a separate heatproof bowl set over a pan of simmering water. Whisk continuously with a balloon whisk until the mixture reaches 71°C on a sugar thermometer.

6. Transfer the egg-white mixture to a stand mixer fitted with the whisk, then whisk on high speed for 5–7 minutes, until you have a stiff, glossy meringue. Add the vanilla paste and salt and whisk for a few seconds to combine. Leave to cool to room temperature.

7. In a separate bowl, whisk the softened butter until light and fluffy, then whisk in the white chocolate ganache until smooth. Add one third of the meringue and whisk gently until the meringue has been incorporated. Gently fold in the remaining meringue. Cover and set aside at room temperature.

Continues overleaf

8. Using a mandoline or very sharp knife, cut the strawberries into wafer-thin slices and place them on kitchen paper.

9. Make the crêpes. Heat the 30cm crêpe or frying pan over a medium heat. Lightly brush with sunflower oil, then remove any excess with scrunched-up kitchen paper.

10. Pour in just enough batter to lightly cover the base of the pan and cook over a medium heat for 1½–2 minutes, until the outside edge begins to crisp. Loosen with a spatula, flip over and cook the other side for another 30 seconds. Transfer the crêpe to a sheet of baking paper and leave to cool.

11. Heat the 24cm crêpe or frying pan over a medium heat and repeat steps 9 and 10 until you have used all the batter. You should end up with 1 large crêpe and 13 smaller ones.

12. Using a 20cm plate or cake-tin base as a guide, trim the 13 smaller pancakes so that they are all the same size.

13. To assemble, cut two 50 x 10cm-long strips of baking paper and arrange them in a cross on the work surface. Place the largest crêpe in the middle of the paper cross. Spoon 2–3 tablespoons of the white chocolate filling on top and spread out evenly with a palette knife.

14. Place one of the smaller crêpes on top of the large crêpe, in the middle, and spread with more filling, then place another crêpe on top. Spread the crêpe with more filling, then neatly arrange a layer of the sliced strawberries over the top, leaving a 1cm border around the edge.

15. Continue layering the crêpes in the same way, adding a layer of strawberries after every second crêpe. You should end up with 7 layers of 2 crêpes and 6 layers of sliced strawberries.

16. Holding the ends of the paper cross, bring them up and over the crêpe cake to meet in the middle, then use as a handle to lift the cake into the lined bowl. Slip the strips of paper out from under the cake.

17. Wrap the cling film tightly over the top (which will become the bottom) of the cake and secure tightly, so the edges of the large crêpe envelop the small crêpes. Chill for at least 4 hours, until set.

18. To serve, turn out the cake, dome-side up, onto a cake plate or cake stand and discard the cling film. Dust with extra matcha powder and decorate with a crescent of fresh fruit, freeze-dried raspberries, desiccated coconut and edible flowers.

FOR THE APPLE PURÉE
2 small eating apples,
    peeled, cored and sliced

FOR THE SPONGE
100g pecans
3 ripe, but not overripe,
    bananas
180ml vegetable oil
160g light brown soft sugar
150g golden caster sugar
1 tsp vanilla paste
330g plain flour
1½ tsp baking powder
1½ tsp bicarbonate of soda
2 tsp ground cinnamon
½ tsp freshly grated nutmeg
30ml almond milk
200g drained canned
    pineapple, crushed

FOR THE CARAMEL SAUCE
50ml canned coconut milk
    or coconut cream
75g light brown soft sugar
½ tbsp golden syrup
¼ tsp vanilla paste
½ tsp cornflour

FOR THE VANILLA FROSTING
400g icing sugar, sifted
125g vegan spread
1 tsp vanilla paste
1 tbsp almond milk, if needed

TO DECORATE
2–3 slices pineapple,
    cut into thin triangles
24 blueberries
2 passion fruit,
    cut into wedges
10 mint leaves
5 pecans, finely chopped

YOU WILL NEED
20cm sandwich tins x 3,
    oiled, then base-lined
    with baking paper
1 small piping bag fitted
    with a large writing nozzle
1 medium piping bag fitted
    with a large plain nozzle
25cm plate or cake board

Serves
12

Hands on
50 mins

Bake
30 mins

Hummingbird Cake

This vegan version of the fruity, lightly spiced layer cake retains all the flavours of the original Jamaican recipe and the more-recent southern American version. The sweet, tropical notes of the fruit, the nuttiness of toasted pecans and the aromatic scent of the spices is why this cake is said to attract hummingbirds.

1. Make the apple purée. Place the apples in a pan with 1 tablespoon of water. Cook over a low heat, simmering for 10 minutes, until soft. Leave to cool slightly, then blitz with a hand-held stick blender or in a food processor to purée. Measure out 150g of the purée and set aside.

2. Heat the oven to 180°C/160°C fan/Gas 4.

3. Make the sponge. Spread the pecans out on a baking tray and toast in the oven for 7 minutes. Leave to cool, then roughly chop. Peel and mash the bananas, then measure out 270g.

4. Pour the oil into the bowl of a stand mixer fitted with the whisk. Add the brown sugar, caster sugar, vanilla, banana and apple purée and whisk, on medium speed for 2 minutes, until combined.

5. Remove the bowl from the mixer, then sift in the flour, baking powder, bicarbonate of soda, cinnamon and nutmeg, then gently fold to a thick batter. Add the almond milk, pineapple and toasted pecans and fold gently. Do not over-mix. Divide the mixture equally between the lined sandwich tins and level with a palette knife.

6. Bake two sponges on the middle shelf and the other on the top shelf for 25–30 minutes, until well risen, dark toffee colour, and a skewer inserted into the centres comes out clean. Remove from the oven and leave in the tins to cool completely.

7. Make the caramel sauce. Reserve 2 teaspoons of the coconut milk or cream and place the remainder in a small pan. Add the sugar, syrup and vanilla. Cook over a low heat, stirring, until the sugar dissolves.

Continues overleaf

8. Mix the cornflour with the reserved coconut milk or cream to a creamy paste, then whisk into the hot sauce. Bring to the boil, reduce the heat and simmer for 5 minutes, until the sauce has reduced by about half to a thick, syrupy consistency. Leave to cool, then pour into the small piping bag.

9. Make the vanilla frosting. Beat the icing sugar, vegan spread and vanilla paste in a stand mixer fitted with the beater, on medium speed for 2–3 minutes, until pale and creamy, adding a little almond milk to loosen if necessary. Spoon into the large piping bag.

10. Turn the sponges out of the tins. Secure the first sponge on the plate or cake board with a little frosting. Pipe some frosting over the top, then pipe a drizzle of caramel over that. Place the next sponge on top of the cake and repeat with the frosting and caramel. Top with the final sponge and pipe a thick layer of frosting over the top of the cake to finish.

11. Using an offset palette knife, create a swirl effect in the frosting and then pipe a swirl of caramel into the frosting. Decorate with the fresh pineapple, blueberries, passion fruit, mint leaves, and chopped pecans. Serve with any remaining caramel alongside.

FOR THE SPONGE
50g unsalted butter
7 eggs
150g caster sugar
1 tsp vanilla extract
  or paste
50g plain flour
40g ground almonds
40g cocoa powder
1 tsp baking powder
pinch of salt

FOR THE CHOCOLATE
MERINGUE BUTTERCREAM
300g 70% dark chocolate,
  chopped
175g caster sugar
3 egg whites
pinch of salt
250g unsalted butter,
  softened

FOR THE CHOCOLATE BARK
200g 70% dark chocolate,
  chopped

TO DECORATE
redcurrants
Christmas-themed
  decorations (optional)
icing sugar, for dusting

YOU WILL NEED
30 x 40cm Swiss roll tin,
  greased, then lined
  (base and sides)
  with baking paper
2 baking sheets, lined
  with baking paper

Serves
10

Hands on
1 ½ hours

Bake
14 mins

plus chilling

Christmas Log Cake

This is a sumptuous twist on a classic yule log, with the layers running vertically rather than horizontally. It looks impressive on any festive table. We like the robins on the top of our cake, but use any Christmas-themed decorations you like, or even just berries.

1. Heat the oven to 180°C/160°C fan/Gas 4.

2. Make the sponge. Melt the butter and set aside to cool slightly. Whisk the eggs, sugar and vanilla in a stand mixer fitted with the whisk until thick and mousse-like, and the mixture leaves a ribbon trail when you lift the whisk.

3. Sift together the flour, ground almonds, cocoa powder, baking powder and salt into the bowl, then gently fold in using a large metal spoon, taking care not to knock out too much air. Add the melted butter and fold again until the mixture is smooth and combined.

4. Carefully pour the mixture into the lined tin and level with a palette knife. Bake on the middle shelf for 12–14 minutes, until the cake is well risen and springy and a skewer inserted into the centre comes out clean.

5. Cool in the tin for 2 minutes, then turn out onto a clean tea towel. Peel off the baking paper and, starting from one of the short ends, roll the sponge into a spiral with the tea towel rolled inside. Leave to cool.

6. Meanwhile, make the chocolate meringue buttercream. Melt the chocolate in a heatproof bowl set over a pan of barely simmering water. Stir until smooth, then remove from the heat.

7. Put the sugar, egg whites and salt into a medium heatproof bowl set over a pan of simmering water. Whisk until the sugar dissolves and the mixture is foamy. Continue to cook for about 3 minutes, whisking continuously, until the mixture thickens and increases in volume, turns from opaque to bright white, and leaves a ribbon trail when you lift the whisk.

Continues overleaf

8. Pour the mixture into the bowl of a stand mixer fitted with the whisk and beat, on medium–high speed for 3–4 minutes, until the mixture doubles in volume and is thick, stiff, glossy and cold to the touch.

9. Gradually, add the butter to the cooled meringue mixture, beating continuously until smooth. Fold in the melted chocolate, then cover until ready to use.

10. Carefully unroll the sponge cake. Turn it so that a long side is closest to you, then cut the cake horizontally into three long strips, each strip about 40 x 10cm. Spread each with 3–4 tablespoons of the meringue buttercream.

11. Roll one strip into a tight Swiss-roll shape. Place the end of the roll at one end of the second iced cake strip, then roll this around the first rolled strip – the cake starts to become a short, wide Swiss roll. Position the end of the roll at one end of the third iced strip and roll again. Carefully turn the cake over and place spiral-side down in the middle of a serving plate. Cover, then chill for 30 minutes.

12. Meanwhile, make the bark. Melt the dark chocolate in a heatproof bowl set over a pan of barely simmering water. Stir until smooth and remove from the heat. Leave to cool for 30 minutes.

13. Measure the height of the cake and draw two parallel lines on each sheet of baking paper lining the baking sheets, positioning them the same distance apart as the height of the cake. Flip the paper over so that you can see the lines through the paper.

14. Re-melt the chocolate until runny again, then spoon it onto the baking paper between the lines. Spread level with a palette knife and leave to cool (not the fridge) until the chocolate starts to set and loses its shine. Using a fork, mark ridges in the chocolate to resemble bark and leave to set solid.

15. Cover the top and sides of the cake with the remaining buttercream. Using a palette knife, spread the sides smoothly and create a swirl pattern on top to resemble the rings of a log.

16. Using a hot knife, cut the chocolate bark into 3cm-wide strips and, using a palette knife, carefully position the bark pieces all around the outside of the cake, pressing them to stick. Decorate the cake with berries and Christmassy cake decorations, then lightly dust with icing sugar. (If you make ahead, leave the cake to come up to room temperature for 30 minutes, before serving.)

Just Because

Recipes

8 eating apples, such as
    Braeburn, Jazz, Granny
    Smith or Golden
    Delicious, peeled, cored,
    and cut into 2–3mm slices
100g caster or vanilla sugar,
    plus 7 tsp for sprinkling
3 tbsp Armagnac or
    Calvados
2 tsp lemon juice
7 sheets filo pastry
75g unsalted butter, melted
300ml double cream
    or crème fraîche
icing sugar, for dusting

YOU WILL NEED
20cm round metal pie tin
    (solid base), brushed
    with melted butter

Serves
6–8

Hands on
30 mins
plus macerating

Bake
45 mins

Pastis Gascon

*This simple-to-make French apple tart is one to round off a
warming meal on a chilly day. Serve it hot or at room temperature,
so that the filo pastry still has its crunch. Substitute the Armagnac
for dry apple cider or even apple juice, if you prefer.*

1. Tip the apples into a large bowl. Add the sugar, Armagnac and
lemon juice and mix well to combine. Cover and leave for 1 hour.
Stir the apples, cover and leave for another 1 hour, until softened.
Tip the apples into a sieve over a bowl to catch the juices, and reserve.

2. Heat the oven to 190°C/170°C fan/Gas 5.

3. Unroll the filo pastry, brush the top sheet with melted butter, then
sprinkle with 1 teaspoon of the extra sugar. Lay the buttered filo sheet
into the pie tin, sugar-side up, press into the base and sides and allow
the excess pastry to hang over the edge. Brush a second sheet of filo,
sprinkle with sugar and place in the tin at an angle to the first sheet.
Continue layering until there are 5 sheets of pastry evenly covering
the base and sides of the tin.

4. Arrange the drained apple slices in the lined tin. Fold the excess
pastry from the top 2 filo sheets over the apples to encase the filling.
Using scissors, trim the rest of the excess pastry. Lightly scrunch
the trimmings and arrange on top.

5. Brush the remaining 2 filo sheets with butter, sprinkle with sugar,
then scrunch into ruffles and place on top of the tart to cover. Bake
on the middle shelf for 10 minutes, then reduce the heat to 180°C/
160°C fan/Gas 4 and cook for another 30–35 minutes, until crisp.

6. Meanwhile, pour the reserved juice from the apples into a small
pan and bring to the boil over a medium heat. Cook until reduced
to a syrup – there should be about 2 tablespoons. Leave to cool.

7. Whip the double cream or crème fraîche to soft peaks, then fold
in the cooled syrup. Serve the tart dusted with icing sugar, with the
whipped cream alongside.

Serves
6-8

Hands on
40 mins

Bake
50 mins

plus chilling

FOR THE PASTRY
225g plain flour
pinch of salt
125g unsalted butter,
    cubed and chilled
50g icing sugar, sifted
1 egg, separated
2–2½ tbsp ice-cold water
2 tsp lemon juice

FOR THE FILLING
6 egg yolks (save the
    whites for the meringue)
150g caster sugar
2 tbsp cornflour
6 passion fruit, cut in
    half and scooped out
finely grated zest and juice
    of 1 unwaxed lemon
finely grated zest and juice
    of 2 unwaxed limes
100g unsalted butter,
    softened
pinch of salt

FOR THE MERINGUE
6 egg whites (reserved
    from the filling)
pinch of salt
300g caster sugar
1 tbsp cornflour
double cream, to serve
    (optional)

YOU WILL NEED
20cm loose-bottomed
    tart tin
baking sheet
baking beans or rice

Lemon, Lime and Passion Fruit Meringue Pie

There's something deeply satisfying about making the elements for this twist on a classic lemon meringue pie. Crispy pastry, smooth curd and fluffy meringue, each with their own specific processes and techniques, come together into a rich, decadent whole. Enjoy it in hearty slices – with double cream, if you wish.

1. Make the pastry. Tip the flour and salt into a mixing bowl and rub in the cubes of butter with your fingertips until the mixture resembles fine breadcrumbs. Add the icing sugar and mix to combine.

2. Make a well in the centre and add the egg yolk, water and lemon juice. Using a round-bladed butter or palette knife, cut through the mixture to combine the ingredients and bring the dough together.

3. Using your hands, knead the dough into a neat ball, then flatten into a disc, cover and chill for 2 hours.

4. Lightly flour your work surface and roll out the pastry until about 3mm thick and large enough to line the base and sides of the tart tin. Line the tin with the pastry, pressing it neatly into the corners and grooves. Trim the excess, prick the base with a fork and chill again for 30 minutes.

5. Heat the oven to 180°C/160°C fan/Gas 4 and place a solid baking sheet on the middle shelf to heat up at the same time.

6. Line the pastry case with scrunched-up baking paper and fill with baking beans or rice. Place the tin on the hot baking sheet and bake for 20–25 minutes, until the edges start to turn crisp and golden. Remove the paper and beans or rice and bake for a further 4–5 minutes to cook the base.

Continues overleaf

7. Lightly beat the egg white and brush it over the base of the pastry in a thin layer and return to the oven for 1 minute – the egg white forms a seal between the pastry and filling.

8. Meanwhile, make the filling. In a medium bowl, whisk together the egg yolks, caster sugar and cornflour until combined and smooth.

9. Sieve the passion fruit into a saucepan, using the back of a wooden spoon to press the seeds and extract as much pulp and juice as possible, then discard the seeds. Add the lemon and lime juice and 150ml water to the pan.

10. Heat the fruit-juice mixture over a medium heat until just boiling. Pour this into the egg-yolk mixture, whisking continuously, until smooth and thoroughly combined. Return the mixture to the pan and cook, whisking, until just boiling, smooth and thickened. You should not be able to taste the cornflour at this stage.

11. Remove the pan from the heat, add the lemon and lime zest, and the butter and salt and whisk until combined and smooth. Pour into the pastry case, spread level and return to the oven for 3–4 minutes, until set. Leave to cool. (Leave the oven on.)

12. Make the meringue. Whisk the egg whites and salt in a stand mixer fitted with the whisk on medium speed until the egg whites just hold stiff peaks.

13. Increase the speed to high and add the sugar, 2 tablespoons at a time, whisking thoroughly between each addition. Continue until you have added all the sugar and the meringue is silky smooth. Add the cornflour and whisk briefly to combine. Spoon the meringue on top of the pie filling, spreading it out with generous swirls.

14. Bake the pie on the hot baking sheet for 15 minutes, until the meringue is golden and the top crisp. Leave to cool to room temperature before serving.

FOR THE FILLING

1.8kg whole chicken
2 onions, cut in half
    lengthways
2 celery sticks, quartered
1 large carrot, quartered
2 bay leaves
4 black peppercorns
2 large leeks, thickly sliced

FOR THE PASTRY

350g plain flour
½ tsp salt
175g unsalted butter,
    cubed and chilled
50g lard, cubed and chilled
¼ tsp English mustard
    powder
good pinch of cayenne
    pepper
½ tsp freshly ground
    black pepper
4–5 tbsp ice-cold water
2 tsp white wine vinegar
    or cider vinegar
1 egg yolk
1 tbsp whole milk

FOR THE SAUCE

50g unsalted butter
50g plain flour
100ml double cream
    or crème fraîche
1 tbsp Dijon mustard
2 rounded tbsp chopped
    flat-leaf parsley
1 tbsp chopped tarragon

YOU WILL NEED

20cm round metal pie tin

Serves
6

Hands on
2 hours
plus chilling

Bake
1 hour

Chicken and Leek Pie

There's almost nothing that says comfort food more than chicken pie. This is a recipe for a lazy Sunday when you have plenty of time. Poaching the chicken and using the stock for the sauce makes good kitchen sense and means that the chicken is tender and the sauce flavoursome. Serve with a big bowl of steamed greens or cabbage.

1. Start the filling by poaching the chicken. Place the chicken in a large saucepan. Add the onions, celery, carrot, bay leaves and peppercorns, then pour in enough cold water to cover by about 3cm. Place the pan over a medium heat and bring to the boil. Reduce the heat to a very gentle simmer, half-cover the pan with a lid, and cook for 40 minutes, until cooked through. Remove from the heat and leave the chicken to cool in the poaching liquid. When cool, cover the pan and place in the fridge until needed (you can leave it overnight).

2. Lift the cold chicken and the onion halves from the pan, saving the poaching liquid. Strip the meat from the chicken in as large pieces as possible and roughly chop the onions, then cover and chill until needed. Discard the chicken skin and return the bones to the pan with the poaching liquid. Bring to the boil on a medium heat, then reduce the heat and simmer for 1 hour, using a slotted spoon to remove any scum that rises to the surface of the stock.

3. Strain the stock into another pan and discard the bones and veg. Return the pan to the heat and continue to simmer the stock until it has reduced to 500ml. Set aside until you make the sauce.

4. While the stock is reducing, make the pastry. Tip the flour and salt into a large mixing bowl. Using your fingertips, rub the butter and lard into the flour until the mixture resembles fine breadcrumbs. Add the mustard, and cayenne and black peppers, then mix to combine.

5. Make a well in the centre, add 4 tablespoons of the ice-cold water and add the vinegar and mix with a palette knife to bring the dough together. Add a little more of the water, if needed.

Continues overleaf

6. Using your hands, gather the dough into a ball. Cut the pastry in half, flatten each piece into a disc, then cover and chill for 2 hours.

7. Meanwhile, make the sauce. Melt the butter in a pan over a medium heat, add the flour and cook, stirring frequently, for 1 minute, until it smells biscuity. Gradually add the reduced stock, whisking continuously until smooth. Reduce the heat and simmer gently for 10 minutes, whisking from time to time, until thickened, glossy and smooth. Add the double cream or crème fraîche, simmer for another 1 minute, then mix in the mustard and both chopped herbs. Season well with salt and pepper. Leave to cool.

8. Finish the pie filling. Steam the leeks for 1 minute, or until just tender. Drain well and pat dry on kitchen paper, then leave to cool. Add the chicken, onions and leeks to the cooled sauce, mix to combine, cover and chill until needed.

9. Heat the oven to 200°C/180°C fan/Gas 6.

10. Lightly dust the work surface with flour and roll out one piece of the chilled pastry into a neat disc, 3–4cm larger than the pie tin and about 3mm thick. Line the pie tin with the pastry, pressing it neatly into the edges and up the sides, leaving the excess hanging over the edge. Spoon the cooled filling into the pastry case. Brush the edge of the pastry with cold water.

11. Roll out the remaining pastry and carefully place it on top of the pie, covering the filling. Press the edges together to seal and trim off any excess, reserving the trimmings. Crimp the pastry edges together between your fingers.

12. Use the pastry trimmings to cut leaf shapes, then brush them with water and press them onto the top of the pie, as you wish. Cut a slit or small cross into the top of the pie to allow steam to escape. Beat together the egg yolk and milk and brush the mixture over the pastry.

13. Place the pie on a baking sheet and bake on the middle shelf for 45 minutes–1 hour, until the pastry is crisp and golden brown and the filling is bubbling. Leave to rest for 2 minutes, then serve with a big bowl of steamed cabbage or other steamed greens.

FOR THE SOURED-CREAM SPONGE
175g unsalted butter
400g plain flour
250g golden caster sugar
100g light muscovado sugar
50g cocoa powder
2 tsp baking powder
1 tsp bicarbonate of soda
½ tsp salt
3 large eggs
150ml soured cream
1 tbsp vanilla extract
125ml sunflower oil

FOR THE WHISKED SPONGE
6 eggs
250g caster sugar
150g unsalted butter
100g plain flour
60g cocoa powder

FOR THE FILLING & SIDES
100g morello cherry jam
390g jar of cherries
    in kirsch
750ml double cream
2 tbsp icing sugar
200g 54% dark chocolate,
    very finely grated

TO DECORATE
75g 70% dark chocolate
75g white chocolate
200g cherries

YOU WILL NEED
20cm round cake tins x 2,
    greased, then base-lined
    with baking paper
1 large piping bag fitted
    with a large star nozzle
1 baking sheet, lined with
    baking paper
2 small paper piping bags

BAKER'S FAVOURITE

Lottie's Black Forest Gâteau

This gâteau is a retro family favourite in our house. It is an intensely chocolatey cherry combo that seems to please all demographics, from the 'I-remember-these-from-the-70s' types to the 'I-hate-cherries-but-this-is-alright' types. Just make sure to serve with a fork to hand; it tends to be too messy for fingers.

1. Heat the oven to 180°C/160°C fan/Gas 4.

2. Make the soured-cream sponge. Melt the butter in a pan over a low heat, then remove from the heat and leave to cool.

3. Meanwhile, mix together the flour, both types of sugar, and the cocoa powder, baking powder, bicarbonate of soda and salt in a large mixing bowl until combined. Using an electric hand whisk, whisk the eggs, soured cream and vanilla in another mixing bowl until fluffy.

4. Using the same hand whisk, mix the sunflower oil into the cooled butter, then whisk in 300ml water to form an emulsion. Gradually, pour in the egg and soured-cream mixture, whisking until smooth. Pour the wet ingredients into the dry, and whisk again until smooth.

5. Divide the mixture equally between the lined cake tins and level with a palette knife.

6. Bake for 40–45 minutes, until risen, firm to the touch and a skewer inserted into the centres comes out clean. Leave to cool in the tins for 10 minutes, then turn out onto a wire rack to cool completely.

7. Make the whisked sponge. Grease and re-line the cake tins. Whisk the eggs and sugar in a stand mixer fitted with the whisk, on high speed for about 10 minutes, until thick and mousse-like and the mixture leaves a ribbon trail when you lift the whisk.

Continues overleaf

8. Meanwhile, melt the butter in a pan over a low heat, then remove from the heat and leave to cool.

9. In a separate bowl, sift together the flour and cocoa powder. Using a large metal spoon, gently fold this into the egg mixture, taking care not to knock out the air. Gently pour the cooled melted butter down the inside of the bowl and carefully fold in.

10. Divide the mixture equally between the lined tins. Bake for 20–25 minutes, until springy to the touch. Leave to cool for 5 minutes, then turn out onto a wire rack to cool completely.

11. Meanwhile, make the filling. Heat the jam in a small pan until melted. Drain the cherries (reserving the juice), chop them a little and stir into the jam. Set aside to cool completely. Pour the juice into a small pan and bring to the boil. Boil for about 5 minutes, or until the syrup is reduced to about 4 tablespoons. Brush 1 tablespoon of the syrup over the top of each cake.

12. Whip 550ml of the cream with the icing sugar to soft peaks.

13. Place 1 soured-cream sponge on a plate, spread with jam and a little cream, then top with a whisked sponge and repeat the jam and cream. Place the second soured-cream sponge on top and repeat, finishing with the last whisked sponge (use the most attractive, flattest cake for the top). Using a palette knife, spread the remaining whipped cream around the sides, but not the top of the cake.

14. Place the finely grated chocolate on a dinner plate. Carefully, holding the top and bottom of the cake, lift it and roll the sides in the grated chocolate until coated.

15. Whip the remaining cream to soft peaks. Spread a little on top of the cake to cover and spoon the remainder into the piping bag with the star nozzle. Pipe rosettes of cream around the top edge.

16. To decorate, melt the white and dark chocolates separately in small heatproof bowls set over small pans of barely simmering water. Dip half the cherries in white chocolate and half in dark. Place on the lined baking sheet and chill for 5 minutes, until set.

17. Pour the remaining melted white and dark chocolate into separate paper piping bags and snip off the ends. Drizzle the white chocolate cherries with dark chocolate and the dark chocolate cherries with white. Chill for 10 minutes, until set, then arrange on top of the cake.

FOR THE ROLLS

500g strong white
    bread flour
50g caster sugar
7g fast-action dried yeast
large pinch of salt
200ml whole milk,
    plus extra for glazing
100g unsalted butter,
    softened
2 eggs, beaten

FOR THE PEAR FILLING

6 small or 4 large ripe
    pears, peeled, cored
    and roughly chopped
1 tbsp caster sugar
juice of ½ lemon
25g unsalted butter
25g 70% dark chocolate,
    coarsely grated, to scatter

FOR THE CINNAMON BUTTER

100g unsalted butter,
    softened
75g light brown soft sugar
1 tbsp ground cinnamon

FOR THE TOFFEE GLAZE

75g unsalted butter
3 tbsp golden syrup
3 tbsp light brown soft sugar

YOU WILL NEED

30 x 20cm baking tin
    (at least 4cm deep),
    greased, then lined
    (base and sides)
    with baking paper

Makes 12

Hands on 45 mins

Bake 35 mins

plus rising

Sticky Pear and Cinnamon Buns

There's something intrinsically meditative about a spiral. These buttery buns are filled with sweet pears, cinnamon butter and a touch of dark chocolate, then drenched in a sticky toffee glaze. Enjoy them during me-time with a large mug of tea or coffee.

1. To make the rolls, combine the flour, sugar, yeast and salt in a stand mixer fitted with the dough hook.

2. Gently warm the milk in a small pan over a low heat. Stir the butter into the pan and pour the mixture into the mixer bowl. Add the beaten eggs. Mix until combined, then knead, on low–medium speed for 6–8 minutes, until the dough is smooth and elastic.

3. Form the dough into a ball, return to the bowl and cover. Leave to rise in a warm place for 1–1½ hours, until doubled in size.

4. Make the pear filling. Tip the pears into a pan with the sugar, lemon juice and butter. Cover and cook over a low–medium heat, stirring from time to time, until the pears are soft and starting to break down and reduce to a purée. Remove the lid to cook off any excess liquid. Remove from the heat and leave to cool.

5. Make the cinnamon butter. Beat the butter, sugar and cinnamon until smooth and creamy.

6. Turn out the dough onto a work surface and knead lightly for 30 seconds. Cover with an upturned bowl and leave to relax for 5 minutes.

7. Lightly flour the work surface and roll out the dough into a neat 50 x 30cm rectangle, with a long side closest to you.

Continues overleaf

8. Spread the cinnamon butter over the dough, leaving a 1cm border around the edge. Spread the pears over the top and scatter with the grated chocolate.

9. Starting at the side closest to you, roll up the dough into a neat spiral, keeping the roll even and tight. Cut the roll along its length into 12 equal slices and place the slices cut-sides up in the lined tin. Cover loosely and leave to prove in a warm place for about 30 minutes, until almost doubled in size.

10. Heat the oven to 180°C/160°C fan/Gas 4. Bake the buns for 25 minutes, until golden brown and well risen.

11. While the buns are baking, prepare the toffee glaze. Gently stir the butter, syrup and sugar together in a small pan over a low–medium heat. Bring to the boil and simmer for about 2 minutes, stirring, until slightly thickened. Set aside.

12. Remove the buns from the oven and spoon the toffee sauce over. Return them to the oven for another 5–10 minutes, until sticky and deep golden. Serve warm or at room temperature.

FOR THE PRALINE CREAM

125g caster sugar
50g blanched hazelnuts, toasted
350ml whole milk
3 egg yolks
25g cornflour
50g unsalted butter, cubed and softened
50g 70% dark chocolate, finely chopped
300ml double cream

FOR THE CRAQUELIN

40g unsalted butter, softened
50g caster sugar
50g plain flour
pinch of salt
1 tbsp icing sugar, plus extra for dusting

FOR THE CHOUX PASTRY

100ml whole milk
75g unsalted butter, cubed and softened
1 tsp caster sugar
pinch of salt
125g plain flour, sifted
4 eggs, lightly beaten

YOU WILL NEED

2 baking sheets, lined
6–7cm and 3cm round cutters
2 sheets of baking paper, each drawn with four 6–7cm-diameter circles (use the cutter as a guide)
large piping bag fitted with a large open star nozzle

Makes
8

Hands on
2 hours
plus chilling

Bake
25 mins

Paris-Brest

Make these filled choux rings when you have plenty of time to enjoy the process – from the indulgent praline-cream filling to the soft choux pastry with a satisfying craquelin crunch. You can make the various elements in stages over a day or so – then, bring them together in a decadent show of well-deserved self-appreciation.

1. Make the praline. Tip 50g of the caster sugar into a heavy-based saucepan and cook, swirling the pan (don't stir) over a low heat to dissolve the sugar until you have a rich, amber-coloured caramel. Working quickly, add the toasted hazelnuts and stir to coat. Tip the caramel-coated nuts onto a lined baking sheet and leave to cool and set. There's no need to wash the pan.

2. Heat the milk in the pan over a medium heat to just below boiling point. In a heatproof bowl, whisk the egg yolks with the remaining 75g sugar and the cornflour until smooth and slightly paler in colour.

3. Pour the hot milk over the egg mixture, whisking continuously until smooth. Return the mixture to the pan and cook, whisking over a medium heat until it comes to the boil, then continue whisking for another 1 minute to cook out the eggs and cornflour.

4. Remove the pan from the heat, add the butter and chocolate and stir until smooth. Pour into a bowl and cover the surface of the custard with a piece of baking paper to prevent a skin forming. Leave to cool, then chill until ready to use.

5. Break the hazelnut praline into pieces, then blitz in a food processor until very finely chopped. Store in an airtight box until needed.

6. Make the craquelin. Beat the butter and sugar with a wooden spoon until smooth. Add the flour and salt and mix to bring together. Using your hands, very lightly knead the dough until smooth. Flatten into a disc, then roll the mixture between two sheets of baking paper until 1–2mm thick. Chill for 30 minutes, until firm.

Continues overleaf

7. Remove the top layer of baking paper and, using the large cutter, stamp out 4 discs from the chilled dough, then use the small cutter to stamp out a hole from the middle of each. Place the rings on a baking sheet and chill. Re-roll the trimmings between the sheets of baking paper again and chill for 10 minutes, or until firm. Stamp out another 4 rings and place these on the baking sheet in the fridge, too.

8. Heat the oven to 190°C/170°C fan/Gas 5.

9. Make the choux. Heat the milk, 100ml water, and the butter, sugar and salt in a saucepan over a medium heat. Stir to melt the butter, then bring the mixture to a rolling boil. Remove from the heat and quickly add the flour. Beat vigorously until the batter is smooth, then return the pan to a low heat for 20–30 seconds, stirring continuously, until the mixture is glossy and leaves the sides of the pan.

10. Tip the mixture into a large bowl and leave to cool for 5 minutes. Gradually add the beaten eggs, mixing well until the batter is silky smooth and reluctantly drops off the spoon. (You may not need to add the last 2–3 teaspoons of egg.) Scoop the mixture into the piping bag fitted with the open star nozzle. Using the drawn circles on the 2 prepared sheets of baking paper to guide you, pipe the choux batter into neat circles, then slide the paper onto baking sheets and transfer to the fridge to chill for 10 minutes. (Clean the bag and nozzle.)

11. Place 1 craquelin ring on top of each choux ring and dust with icing sugar. Bake on the middle shelves for about 25 minutes, until the buns are golden brown, puffed up and the topping is crumbly. You may need to turn the trays around in the oven for the last 3 minutes to ensure that the buns brown evenly. Leave to cool for 20 minutes.

12. Using a serrated knife, cut each choux ring in half horizontally and remove any uncooked dough from the middle of each ring. Return to the oven, cut-side up, for 1–2 minutes to dry and crisp the insides. Leave to cool completely before filling.

13. To finish the praline cream filling. Whip the double cream to firm peaks, then fold in the chilled crème pâtissière and praline until combined. Spoon into the piping bag fitted with the star nozzle and pipe into the bottom half each choux ring. Place the choux lids on top, dust with extra icing sugar and serve immediately.

225g plain flour
1 tsp baking powder
40g icing sugar, sifted
pinch of salt
125g unsalted butter,
    cubed and chilled
100g full-fat cream
    cheese, chilled
75g ground almonds
2 egg yolks
1½ tbsp ice-cold water
2 tsp lemon juice

FOR THE FILLING
800g plums (about 10),
    quartered and stoned
200g blackberries
4 tbsp golden caster sugar
juice of ½ lemon
1½ tbsp cornflour
1 tsp vanilla paste
1 egg, separated
150ml double cream

YOU WILL NEED
 cast-iron skillet or 25cm
    ovenproof frying pan
    with a 20cm base

*Serves
6–8*

*Hands on
50 mins*

*Bake
1 hour*

plus chilling

Pandowdy Swamp Pie

*Pandowdy is an old-fashioned American pie filled with cooked fruit
and a pastry-crust top. The swamp part is a simple custard that is
poured into the hot pie and cooks into a puddle with the fruit juices.
Don't worry if your lattice skills aren't showstopping: this is comfort
food – the pie has every right to look a little homespun.*

1. Make the cream-cheese pastry. Tip the flour, baking powder,
sugar and salt into a food processor. Add the butter and pulse
until the mixture resembles fine breadcrumbs. Add all the cream
cheese, scooping it in using a teaspoon (to break it up), then pulse
for 10 seconds. Add the almonds, egg yolks, ice-cold water and lemon
juice and mix again until the dough comes together in large clumps.

2. Turn out the dough onto a work surface and, using lightly floured
hands, bring it together into a neat ball, but do not overwork – it will
be wetter and stickier than usual pastry. Flatten it into a disc, then
cover and chill for at least 2 hours.

3. Cut the pastry in half. Wrap one half and return it to the fridge.
Lightly dust the work surface with flour and roll out 1 piece of the
chilled pastry into a neat disc, about 3mm thick and large enough
to line the base and sides of the skillet with a 1cm overhang.

4. Line the skillet with the pastry, pressing it into the edges and up the
sides, leaving the excess to overhang the sides. Chill for 20 minutes.

5. Heat the oven to 190°C/170°C fan/Gas 5.

6. Make the filling. Cut each plum quarter in half again. Tip the pieces
into a bowl, add the blackberries, 3 tablespoons of the sugar, and the
lemon juice, cornflour and vanilla paste and mix well to combine.
Scoop the filling and any residual juices into the pastry-lined skillet.

Continues overleaf

7. Remove the remaining pastry half from the fridge. Roll it out on a lightly floured work surface to a neat disc, about 3mm thick and a little larger than the top of the skillet.

8. Cut the pastry into eight 3–4cm-wide strips. Lattice the strips on top of the fruit, interweaving them under and over each other, and leaving gaps here and there for the steam to escape and to pour in the cream mixture later. Trim any excess pastry and crimp the edges to seal.

9. Lightly beat the egg white, brush it over the pastry and scatter with the remaining 1 tablespoon of sugar.

10. Place the pie on a baking sheet and bake on the middle shelf for 20 minutes, then reduce the temperature to 180°C/160°C fan/ Gas 4. Turn the pie around and cook for another 30–35 minutes, until the pastry is crisp and golden brown and the fruit filling is tender and bubbling.

11. Whisk together the cream and egg yolk. After the 30–35 minutes, carefully pour the cream mixture into the pie through the gaps in the lattice top. Don't worry if some floods over the top of the pastry – this is what makes the pie swampy. Bake for another 10 minutes, or until the custard sets, then remove from the oven and serve hot.

FOR THE SYRUP
130g caster sugar
65ml just-boiled water
1 lemon wedge

FOR THE FILLING
1 small pineapple
6 maraschino cherries,
    stems removed

FOR THE SPONGE
125g unsalted butter,
    softened
125g caster sugar
2 eggs
125g self-raising flour

**FOR THE CUSTARD
(OPTIONAL)**
675ml whole milk
3 large egg yolks
50g caster sugar
2 tbsp cornflour
1 tsp vanilla extract

TO DECORATE
100ml double cream
6 maraschino cherries,
    with stems

YOU WILL NEED
6cm and 1.5cm round
    cutters
175ml mini pudding
    moulds x 6, greased
medium piping bag fitted
    with a medium closed
    star nozzle

Makes
6

Hands on
1 hour

Bake
25 mins

JUDGE'S RECIPE

Paul's Pineapple Upside-down Cakes

Puddings to make you smile! The homemade golden syrup – which is darker and richer than shop-bought – makes all the difference. There's a double-cherry treat, too – in the filling and in the finish.

1. Make the syrup. Tip 30g of the caster sugar into a small pan and add 2 tablespoons of cold water. Place over a low heat and stir until the sugar dissolves. Increase the heat and cook for 3–5 minutes, until you have a golden, caramel syrup.

2. Remove from the heat and very carefully pour in the just-boiled water (stand back as the caramel will spit a bit). Return to a low heat, add the lemon wedge and remaining 100g sugar, then stir until the mixture comes to the boil. Reduce the heat and simmer very gently for 20 minutes, until you have a light golden colour and a syrupy consistency. Remove from the heat.

3. Meanwhile, prepare the filling. Cut the top and base off the pineapple and carefully cut away the skin from top to bottom. Cut 6 horizontal slices, each about 1cm thick, from the pineapple. Using the 6cm cutter, cut the pineapple slices into neat rounds (eat the trimmings). Using the 1.5cm cutter, cut a hole in the centre of each round to remove the core and make 6 pineapple rings.

4. Divide the syrup equally between the pudding moulds. Place a pineapple ring in each mould and a maraschino cherry in the centre of each pineapple ring. Set aside.

5. Heat the oven to 180°C/160°C fan/Gas 4.

6. Make the sponge. Beat the butter and sugar in a stand mixer fitted with the beater, on medium speed for 3–5 minutes, until pale and creamy, scraping down the sides of the bowl from time to time.

Continues overleaf

7. Add the eggs, one at a time, beating well between each addition. With the mixer on low speed, mix in the flour until just combined.

8. Spoon the sponge batter equally into the moulds and level with the back of the spoon. Bake for 20–25 minutes, until risen, golden and a skewer inserted into the centres comes out clean. Leave to cool in the moulds for 3–5 minutes, then turn out onto a wire rack to cool completely.

9. Make the custard. Heat the milk in a heavy-based saucepan over a medium heat to just below boiling point.

10. In a large mixing bowl, whisk together the egg yolks, caster sugar, cornflour and vanilla extract with an electric hand whisk until pale and fluffy.

11. Whisking continuously, pour the warmed milk over the egg mixture. Return the mixture to the pan and cook over a very low heat for 3–4 minutes, stirring continuously, until smooth and thick enough to coat the back of a spoon. Remove from the heat and set aside.

12. To decorate, whip the double cream to soft peaks and spoon into the piping bag fitted with a medium closed star nozzle. Pipe a rosette of cream on the top of each pineapple cake and finish with a maraschino cherry with stem. Serve the cakes with the warm custard, if you wish.

Makes
24

Hands on
1 ½ hours
plus chilling

Bake
30 mins

BAKER'S FAVOURITE

Linda's Flaky Black Pudding Sausage Rolls

These sausage rolls are among my family's favourites. They are on the Very Important Pastry list for all our family occasions, but I also make them a couple of times a week (along with cheese straws) just because they are so irresistible.

FOR THE PASTRY
250g unsalted butter
250g plain flour, plus extra for dusting
½ tsp fine sea salt
150ml ice-cold water
1 egg white, to glaze

FOR THE FILLING
150g black pudding, skin removed
500g good-quality pork sausagemeat
¼ tsp garlic purée
pinch each of salt and freshly ground black pepper

1. Make the pastry. Place the block of butter in the freezer for 10 minutes. Sift the flour and salt in a large mixing bowl and place this in the fridge while you prepare the filling.

2. Crumble the black pudding in a medium bowl, add the sausagemeat, garlic and seasoning. Mix well.

3. Tip out the filling mixture onto a floured work surface. Divide it into 4 equal pieces and, using your hands, roll each piece into a 33cm-long sausage shape, about the thickness of a chipolata. Cover and chill while you make the pastry.

4. Take the bowl of flour out of the fridge and, using the coarse side of a box grater, grate in the frozen butter (dip the butter into the flour every now and then to prevent it sticking together as you grate).

5. Using a round-bladed knife and with a chopping motion against the sides of the bowl, mix the butter through the flour. Add the ice-cold water and, working quickly so as not to over-handle the dough, bring the mixture together, then knead lightly into a ball. Flatten slightly, wrap, and chill for 20 minutes.

6. On a lightly floured work surface, roll out the dough into a 15 x 35cm-long rectangle. Fold down the top third of the pastry, then fold up the bottom third of pastry, as if folding a business letter.

Continues overleaf

7. Turn the folded dough through 90° clockwise, then press the edges with a rolling pin and repeat the rolling and folding twice more. Wrap and chill for 20 minutes. Roll and fold twice more, then chill for 1 hour.

8. Halve the chilled pastry block and roll out each half into a rectangle measuring about 18 x 33cm and 3mm thick. Halve each rectangle lengthways so that altogether you have 4 long strips, each about 9cm wide. Trim the short ends to neaten.

9. Remove the 4 rolls of filling from the fridge and place 1 roll into the centre of each strip. Dampen one long edge of each pastry strip with water and fold the pastry over the filling to enclose it completely. Dip a fork into a saucer of flour and use the tines to press the edges to seal.

10. Cut each long sausage roll into 5cm widths, to give you 24 smaller sausage rolls altogether. With a sharp knife score a couple of lines across the middle of each roll. Gently transfer the sausage rolls onto two baking sheets.

11. Brush the rolls with egg white to glaze, then chill for 20 minutes before baking. While the sausage rolls are chilling, preheat the oven to 220°C/200°C fan/Gas 7.

12. Bake the sausage rolls for about 25–30 minutes, until golden brown and crispy, then remove from the oven and transfer to a wire rack to cool. Serve warm or cold.

FOR THE SPONGE
50g cocoa powder
6 tbsp just-boiled water
200g unsalted butter,
    softened
150g caster sugar
125g light brown soft sugar
4 eggs
250g self-raising flour
½ tsp baking powder
pinch of salt
4 tbsp whole milk

FOR THE GANACHE
200g 70% dark chocolate,
    finely chopped
10g unsalted butter,
    at room temperature
300ml double cream
2 tsp caster sugar

TO DECORATE
250g raspberries
icing sugar, to serve

YOU WILL NEED
20cm round cake tins x 2,
    greased, then base-lined
    with baking paper

Serves
10

Hands on
40 mins

Bake
35 mins

Our Chocolate Cake

Chocolate cake, surely, has to be the ultimate 'just because' bake. Inspired by the Bake Off *credits, this one is decadently rich and topped with raspberries. If raspberries aren't in season, use other berries or fruit, or a mountain of chocolate shavings or curls.*

1. Heat the oven to 180°C/160°C fan/Gas 4.

2. Make the sponge. In a small bowl, combine the cocoa with the just-boiled water and mix until smooth.

3. Beat the butter and both sugars in a stand mixer fitted with the beater, on medium speed for 3–5 minutes, or until pale and creamy, scraping down the sides of the bowl from time to time.

4. Add the eggs, one at a time, beating well between each addition. Sift the flour, baking powder and salt into the bowl. Add the cocoa paste and mix again until smooth and nearly combined. Mix in the milk until smooth.

5. Divide the mixture equally between the lined tins and level with a palette knife. Bake on the middle shelf for 30–35 minutes, until well risen, the tops bounce back when lightly pressed, and a skewer inserted into the centres comes out clean. Remove from the oven and cool in the tins on a wire rack for 3–4 minutes, then turn out and leave to cool completely.

6. Meanwhile, make the ganache. Tip the chopped chocolate and the butter into a bowl and set aside. Pour the cream into a saucepan, add the sugar and bring to the boil, stirring occasionally. Remove from the heat, leave to cool for 30 seconds, then pour this over the chocolate. Leave to melt, without stirring, for 1 minute. Using a wooden spoon, stir until smooth, then leave to cool and thicken slightly.

7. Place one sponge on a serving plate and top with 3 tablespoons of ganache, spreading it smoothly with a palette knife. Top with the second sponge, then cover the top and sides with the remaining ganache. Top with raspberries and dust with icing sugar to serve.

500g strong white
bread flour
50g caster sugar, plus
extra for dusting
10.5g fast-action
dried yeast
½ tsp salt
250ml whole milk
75g unsalted butter,
softened
2 eggs, beaten
2 tsp vanilla extract
about 2 litres sunflower oil,
for frying

YOU WILL NEED
7cm and 3cm round cutters
2 large baking sheets,
dusted with flour
2 proving bags
deep-fat fryer or large,
deep saucepan

Makes
10-12

Hands on
30 mins

Fry
30 mins

plus rising

Ring Doughnuts

Sometimes only a doughnut will do. Coated in sugar (or melted chocolate, if you prefer) and eaten warm, is there anything more comforting? Frying the middles as little balls gives you cheeky little doughnut bites, too!

1. Tip the flour into the bowl of a stand mixer fitted with the dough hook. Add the sugar, yeast and salt and mix to combine.

2. Gently warm the milk in a small pan over a low heat. Stir the butter into the pan and pour the mixture into the mixer bowl. Add the eggs and vanilla and mix on a low speed to combine. Increase the speed to medium and knead the dough for 5 minutes, or until smooth, elastic and it starts to come away from the sides of the bowl.

3. Turn out the dough onto a lightly floured work surface and shape into a neat ball. Place in a lightly oiled bowl, cover and leave to rise for 1–2 hours, until doubled in size.

4. Turn out the dough again and knead for 30 seconds to knock out any large air pockets. Dust the work surface with flour and roll out the dough to about 1–2cm thick. Using a floured 7cm cutter, stamp out as many rounds as possible. Use the smaller cutter to stamp out the middle of each round to make a ring. Reserve the middles.

5. Gather the trimmings, knead them lightly, re-roll, then roll and cut out more rings and middles until you have about 10–12 doughnuts.

6. Arrange all the rings and middles on the baking sheets, spacing them well apart. Place each tray of doughnuts in a proving bag and leave to prove for 1 hour, or until doubled in size.

7. Heat the oil in a deep-fat fryer to 180°C (or two-thirds fill a large pan with oil and heat to 180°C). Fry the doughnuts and middles two or three at a time, for about 2 minutes on each side, until golden brown. Remove with a slotted spoon and set aside to drain on kitchen paper. Bring the oil back up to temperature, then fry the next batch. Repeat for all the doughnuts and balls. Dust with caster sugar to serve.

110g self-raising flour,
    plus extra for dusting
50g fresh white
    breadcrumbs
finely grated zest of
    1 small unwaxed lemon
75g vegetable suet
50ml whole milk

FOR THE FILLING
125g unsalted butter, cubed,
    plus extra for greasing
125g light muscovado sugar
1 unwaxed lemon, halved

**FOR THE CRÈME ANGLAISE
(ENOUGH FOR 4 PEOPLE)**
250ml whole milk
250ml double cream
1 vanilla pod, split
    and seeds scraped
6 large egg yolks
65g caster sugar

YOU WILL NEED
285ml mini pudding
    moulds x 2, greased,
    then base-lined with
    greased baking paper
2 circles of baking paper cut
    6cm larger in diameter
    than the rim of 1 mould
2 circles of foil cut 6cm
    larger in diameter than
    the rim of 1 mould
kitchen string

JUDGE'S RECIPE

Prue's Sussex Pond Puddings

Delicious vegetarian suet pastry filled with lemon-flavoured butter and sugar, these little puddings are surely the epitome of Britishness and the very definition of comfort food. Serve them with homemade crème Anglaise in front of a roaring fire. (Each pudding will serve one or two people, depending on appetite.)

1. Sift the flour into a bowl and add the breadcrumbs, lemon zest and suet. Mix the milk with 50ml water, then stir into the flour mixture, to a soft but not sticky dough. Knead for 1–2 minutes, then divide the dough in half.

2. One piece at a time, break off a quarter of the dough half, cover and set aside. Roll out the larger piece on a lightly floured surface until it is 7mm thick and will line the first pudding mould with a 2cm overhang. Line the mould.

3. Repeat with the other half of the dough – breaking off, covering and setting aside one quarter and rolling out three quarters, so that both pudding moulds are lined and you have 2 smaller pieces of dough set aside.

4. Make the filling. In a bowl mix the butter and sugar together, and place one quarter of the mixture in the base of each pudding mould.

5. One lemon half at a time, place the cut side down on the work surface and make two horizontal cuts: one quarter of the way down and three-quarters of the way down the lemon half, cutting almost but not all the way through. Rotate the lemon through 180°, still facing downwards, and make a similar cut halfway down, in the opposite direction to the other two – you'll end up with a concertina-like lemon half. Repeat for the other half. Place 1 lemon half pointed end down in each pastry-lined mould. Cover with the remaining filling.

Continues overleaf

6. Roll out the remaining pastry to make 2 lids, each the same thickness as the base. Brush the pastry around the rim of the moulds with water, then top with the lids and press together firmly to seal.

7. Fold a pleat in the centre of each disc of baking paper and each disc of foil (to give the puddings room to expand), then cover the pudding moulds first with a disc of pleated paper and then with the foil. Secure with string, looping it first around the rim and then across the top to make a handle.

8. Place the moulds, covered sides upwards, in a steamer and steam for 2 hours, topping up the water from time to time, if necessary.

9. About 20 minutes before the end of the cooking time, make the crème Anglaise. Heat the milk, cream and vanilla seeds in a pan over a medium heat to just below boiling point.

10. In a large bowl, whisk the egg yolks and caster sugar together until pale and fluffy. Pour the warmed milk mixture over the egg mixture, whisking continuously until combined.

11. Pour the mixture into a heavy-based pan and cook over a very low heat for 3–4 minutes, stirring continuously, until smooth and thick enough to coat the back of a spoon. Remove from the heat and set aside.

12. When the puddings are ready, use the string handle to carefully remove them from the steamer and leave to cool for 5 minutes. Remove the string, foil and baking paper. Place a serving plate over the top of each pudding mould, then carefully invert the pudding out onto the plate. Serve with the crème Anglaise on the side.

Makes
18

Hands on
1 ½ hours

Bake
30 mins

plus marinating
and chilling

FOR THE FILLING
4 skinless, boneless
   chicken thighs
1 tbsp harissa paste
1 tsp salt
1 tbsp olive oil
1 onion, very finely chopped
1 garlic clove, crushed
2 tbsp ras el hanout
¼ tsp ground cinnamon
½ tsp smoked paprika
½ tbsp plain flour
juice and finely grated zest
   of ½ unwaxed lemon
150ml chicken stock,
   plus extra if needed
50g raisins
4 dried apricots
120g chickpeas from a can
   (drained weight)
30g pitted green olives,
   chopped
1 tbsp chopped coriander
salt and freshly ground
   black pepper

FOR THE SHORTCRUST
PASTRY
500g plain flour, plus
   extra for dusting
250g unsalted butter,
   cubed and chilled
pinch of salt
2 egg yolks
1 egg, lightly beaten

YOU WILL NEED
11cm and 7cm round cutters
12-hole muffin tray, greased
6-hole muffin tray, greased

BAKER'S FAVOURITE

Mark's Chicken Tagine Pies

I started making these mini pies after a trip to Marrakech using ras el hanout that I brought home with me. I love how easy they are with shortcrust pastry (although they're also good with puff). Now, I make them just to remind me of all the tagines I ate on my trip.

1. Start the filling. Place the chicken thighs, harissa paste and salt in a bowl. Mix until the chicken is covered in the paste, then cover and leave to marinate for 30 minutes, or overnight in the fridge if you can.

2. Make the pastry. Place the flour, butter and salt in a food processor. Pulse for 2–3 seconds at a time until the mixture resembles fine breadcrumbs. Add the egg yolks and pulse to combine. Add about 5 tablespoons of water, a tablespoon at a time, until the mixture comes together. Tip the dough onto a lightly floured work surface, bring it together into a ball, then flatten slightly. Wrap and chill until needed.

3. Meanwhile, continue to make the filling. Heat the oil in a pan, add the onion and fry over a low heat for 5–10 minutes, until transparent. Add the garlic and cook for 2–3 minutes, until softened. Stir in the ras el hanout, cinnamon, paprika and flour and cook for 30 seconds.

4. Add the chicken thighs and stir to coat in the onion and spice mixture, then add the lemon juice and zest and the chicken stock, making sure the liquid covers the chicken. Bring to the boil, then reduce the heat, cover with a lid and simmer for 20 minutes, until cooked through and there is no sign of pink meat.

5. Remove the chicken from the pan, shred it with two forks and return it to the pan. Add the raisins, apricots and chickpeas and cook on a low heat for 10 minutes.

Continues overleaf

6. Add the olives and cook for a further 5 minutes, adding more chicken stock if the mixture is too dry – it should be moist, but not too wet. Season with salt and pepper and stir in the coriander. Remove from the heat and leave to cool completely.

7. Remove the pastry from the fridge and leave to soften for 5–10 minutes. Cut off two thirds of the pastry and roll out on a lightly floured work surface until 3mm thick. Using the 11cm cutter, cut out 18 pastry discs and press into the hollows in the muffin tins. Press out any pleats to make the pastry an even thickness all round and trim the tops evenly.

8. Divide the tagine mixture equally between the pastry cases, pressing it down well. Brush the edges of the pastry with a little of the beaten egg.

9. Roll out the remaining pastry on a lightly floured work surface, until about 3mm thick. Using the 7cm cutter, cut out 18 pastry lids, then use a skewer to piece a hole in each or a sharp knife to cut little dashes all over (to allow the steam to escape). Place a lid on top of each pie, pressing the edges together to seal. Brush the tops with the remaining beaten egg and chill for 20 minutes.

10. Meanwhile, heat the oven to 200°C/180°C fan/Gas 6.

11. Bake the pies on the middle shelves for about 30 minutes, until the pastry is crisp and golden. Serve hot or cold.

CHAPTER FIVE

Community

Recipes

RICCIARELLI

KITCHEN SINK COOKIES

PEANUT BUTTER AND RASPBERRY BLONDIES

PAUL'S JAM AND CUSTARD DOUGHNUTS

APRICOT AND ALMOND TARTS

LEMON, LIME AND GINGER DRIZZLE CAKES

PEANUT AND CARAMEL MILLIONAIRE'S SHORTBREAD

SURA'S PARSLEY, FETA AND SPINACH TURKISH PASTRIES

PRUE'S RASPBERRY AND SALTED CARAMEL ÉCLAIRS

STICKY TOFFEE APPLE CAKES

SOURDOUGH

SPECULOOS CHEESECAKE SQUARES

CHEESE AND SPRING ONION SCONES

2 egg whites
pinch of salt
1 tsp lemon juice
225g icing sugar, sifted,
    plus extra for dusting
¼ tsp gluten-free
    baking powder
250g ground almonds
1 tsp finely grated
    unwaxed lemon zest
1 tsp almond extract
½ tsp vanilla paste

YOU WILL NEED
baking sheet, greased, then
    lined with baking paper

Makes
20

Hands on
10 mins

Bake
25 mins

plus resting

Ricciarelli

*These slightly chewy, sticky almond biscuits, from Italy, are similar
to the French macaron – but are much easier to make. We think they
make the perfect bite-sized treat to serve with a cup of coffee or tea
at a street party. Alternatively, wrap them in gift boxes and tie with
a ribbon to sell at a cake sale, or even give away as a gift.*

1. In a clean bowl, whisk the egg whites with the pinch of salt and the
lemon juice until they form stiff peaks. Sift the icing sugar and baking
powder into the bowl, add the ground almonds, lemon zest, almond
extract and vanilla paste and fold in using a large metal spoon or
rubber spatula.

2. Using slightly damp hands, divide the mixture into 20 walnut-sized
balls, then roll each one in extra icing sugar to coat.

3. Arrange the ricciarelli on the lined baking sheet and, using
the fingers of one hand, flatten them slightly to 1–2cm thick. Leave
uncovered at room temperature for about 1 hour, until the outside
of the biscuits dry out slightly.

4. Heat the oven to 150°C/130°C fan/Gas 2.

5. Bake for 25 minutes, until the biscuits are just firm, cracked
and starting to turn pale golden in colour.

6. Remove from the oven and leave to cool on a wire rack. Store
the biscuits in an airtight container lined with baking paper until
you're ready to serve.

225g unsalted butter, softened
200g light brown soft sugar
50g dark brown soft sugar
2 eggs
225g plain flour
1 tsp bicarbonate of soda
pinch of salt
75g rolled porridge oats
100g 70% dark chocolate, roughly chopped
100g white chocolate, roughly chopped
75g milk chocolate, roughly chopped
100g pecans or walnuts, roughly chopped
100g raisins
50g desiccated coconut
75g toffee or fudge pieces

YOU WILL NEED
2 baking sheets, greased, then lined with baking paper

Makes about 24

Hands on 20 mins

Bake 15 mins

plus chilling

Kitchen Sink Cookies

Everything but the kitchen sink... these cookies are chock-a-block with chocolate (three types!), oats, nuts, raisins, coconut and fudge pieces. Choose the nuts and dried fruit according to what you prefer or have in the cupboard – they're an ideal way to use up any open bags, and for when you need to provide something for a last-minute school cake sale or an office bake off.

1. Beat the butter and both sugars in a stand mixer fitted with the beater, on medium speed for 3–5 minutes, until pale and creamy.

2. Add the eggs, one at a time, beating well between each addition until smooth.

3. Sift together the flour, bicarbonate of soda and salt into the bowl, add the oats and mix again until nearly combined.

4. Remove the bowl from the mixer, add all the chopped chocolates, and the nuts, raisins, coconut and toffee or fudge pieces and, using a large spoon, mix together to thoroughly incorporate until all the pieces are evenly distributed.

5. Using an ice-cream scoop or a tablespoon, shape or roll the mixture into 24 neat balls and arrange on the lined baking sheets. Cover and chill for at least 1 hour or up to 24 hours, until firmed up.

6. Heat the oven to 180°C/160°C fan/Gas 4.

7. Bake in batches. Arrange 6 cookies on each lined baking sheet, spacing them well apart, and bake on the middle shelves for 10 minutes. Remove the baking sheets from the oven and tap them sharply on the work surface to deflate the cookies slightly. Return to the oven for a further 5 minutes, until the cookies are golden and starting to turn crisp at the edges.

8. Leave the cookies to cool and firm up on the baking sheets for 5 minutes, then transfer to a wire rack to cool completely. Cook and cool the second batch of cookies in the same way.

125g unsalted butter, cubed

75g roasted unsalted peanuts, roughly chopped, plus extra 1 tbsp (chopped) for sprinkling

200g plain flour, sifted

1 tsp baking powder, sifted

150g light brown soft sugar

50g golden caster sugar

pinch of salt

75g white or dark chocolate chips, or a mixture

1 tbsp freeze-dried raspberry pieces (optional)

75g crunchy or smooth peanut butter, plus 3 tbsp

2 eggs

1 tsp vanilla paste

3 tbsp homemade or good-quality raspberry jam

16 raspberries

YOU WILL NEED

20cm square traybake tin, greased, then lined (base and sides) with baking paper

Peanut Butter and Raspberry Blondies

The middle of each of these blondies is filled with jam and peanut butter, then topped with a fresh raspberry. Ready in under an hour they are a good choice to whip up in an evening and take into the office or share with friends over coffee the following day.

1. Heat the oven to 200°C/180°C fan/Gas 6.

2. Melt the butter in a heavy-based saucepan over a medium–low heat. Continue to heat the melted butter, swirling the pan from time to time for another 2 minutes, until it smells nutty and toasted, and turns golden brown. Tip the butter into a bowl and leave to cool for 3–4 minutes.

3. Meanwhile, tip the peanuts into a bowl with the plain flour, baking powder, light brown soft sugar, caster sugar and pinch of salt and mix to thoroughly combine. Add the chocolate chips and freeze-dried raspberry pieces, if using.

4. Add the 75g peanut butter to the melted butter along with the eggs and vanilla paste and whisk to combine. Add to the dry ingredients and mix to combine. The mixture will be firmer than regular brownies. Spoon into the lined tin and spread level.

5. Using a teaspoon, make 16 evenly spaced indents in the brownie mixture so that there will be one indent in the centre of each blondie. Spoon ½ teaspoon of peanut butter into each indent, followed by ½ teaspoon of raspberry jam. Top the jam with a fresh raspberry and sprinkle over the extra peanuts.

6. Bake for 22–24 minutes, until firm, risen and golden brown. Leave to cool completely before cutting into 16 squares with a raspberry in the middle of each one.

FOR THE DOUGH
125ml whole milk
1 large egg
250g strong white
bread flour
35g unsalted butter,
cubed and softened
5g fast-action dried yeast
5g fine salt
25g caster sugar, plus
extra for coating

FOR THE JAM
100g strawberries,
roughly chopped
100g jam sugar

FOR THE CRÈME MOUSSELINE
250ml whole milk
2 large egg yolks
40g caster sugar
15g plain flour
15g cornflour
1 tsp vanilla extract
pinch of salt
40g unsalted butter,
cubed and chilled
40g unsalted butter,
softened

FOR DEEP FRYING
vegetable oil

YOU WILL NEED
sugar thermometer
deep-fat fryer
large piping bag fitted
with a medium closed
star nozzle
medium piping bag fitted
with a large writing nozzle
proving bag (optional)

Makes
6

Hands on
30 mins

Fry
20 mins

plus rising

JUDGE'S RECIPE

Paul's Jam and Custard Doughnuts

Who wouldn't choose the custard-filled doughnuts in a table full of treats? Sugar-coated with a neat stripe of homemade jam to finish, they are quintessentially British summer fête.

1. Make the dough. Gently warm the milk in a small pan over a low heat. Pour into a jug and beat in the egg.

2. Tip the flour into a mixing bowl and add the butter. Add the yeast to one side of the bowl and the salt and sugar to the other, then stir until combined. Slowly add the milk mixture, stirring by hand to form a dough. Knead in the bowl for about 4 minutes to bring together.

3. Turn out the dough onto a lightly floured work surface, and knead well for about 10 minutes, until the dough is smooth and elastic – it will still be quite sticky at this stage – then place in a clean bowl, cover with a damp tea towel and leave to rise for about 45 minutes, until doubled in size.

4. Meanwhile, make the jam. Put the strawberries in a small saucepan, add the jam sugar and slowly bring to the boil over a low heat. Crush the strawberries and sugar together using a potato masher, then when the sugar melts, increase the heat and boil for another 4 minutes, until the temperature on a sugar thermometer reaches 105°C. Remove from the heat and carefully pass through a sieve to remove the seeds. Leave to cool and set.

5. Meanwhile, make the crème mousseline. Heat the milk over a low heat in a heavy-based pan.

6. In a mixing bowl, whisk the egg yolks and sugar until combined. Sift in the plain flour and cornflour, then whisk until smooth. Whisk in the vanilla extract and salt.

Continues overleaf

7. Pour a quarter of the warm milk onto the egg mixture, whisking continuously, then pour the mixture back into the pan of warm milk. Return the pan to a medium heat and cook, whisking continuously, until the mixture begins to boil. Cook for 2–3 minutes to a thick custard consistency.

8. Remove from the heat and stir in the chilled, cubed butter until combined. Transfer to a heatproof bowl and leave to cool.

9. Meanwhile, beat the softened butter until pale and creamy. When the crème mousseline has cooled to room temperature, add the creamed butter and whisk until smooth.

10. Turn out the dough onto a very lightly floured work surface and knead it a few times to knock it back. Divide the dough into 6 equal portions, about 70g each, and form each portion into a 15cm-long finger shape, with rounded ends.

11. Place the dough fingers onto a floured baking tray and leave to prove, covered (use a proving bag if you have one), for about 30 minutes, until almost doubled in size.

12. Pour enough caster sugar into a wide, shallow bowl to coat the doughnuts and set aside.

13. Half-fill a deep-fat fryer or large, heavy-based pan with vegetable oil and place over a medium heat until it reaches 180°C. In batches of two at a time, carefully lower the doughnuts into the oil and fry for about 3 minutes on each side, until golden brown.

14. Remove the doughnuts with a slotted spoon and immediately roll in the sugar until coated – the hot fat helps the sugar to stick. Set aside and leave to cool while you fry the remainder and coat them in sugar. Leave to cool completely.

15. Using a serrated knife, make a deep cut lengthways down the middle of each cooled doughnut, without slicing fully in half.

16. Spoon the cooled crème mousseline into the large piping bag fitted with the medium closed star nozzle, twist the top to seal, and neatly pipe the custard along the middle of each doughnut.

17. Spoon the cooled jam into the piping bag fitted with a large writing nozzle, twist the top to seal and pipe a line of jam along the middle of the crème mousseline to finish.

Makes
18

Hands on
45 mins

Bake
25 mins

plus chilling

FOR THE PASTRY
250g plain flour, sifted
pinch of salt
150g unsalted butter,
   cubed and chilled
50g icing sugar, sifted,
   plus extra for dusting
35g ground almonds
1 egg, beaten
1½–2 tbsp whole milk

FOR THE FILLING
2 tbsp apricot jam
150g unsalted butter,
   softened
150g caster sugar
2 eggs, lightly beaten
1 egg yolk
100g ground almonds
50g plain flour
½ tsp baking powder
pinch of salt
1 tsp finely grated
   unwaxed lemon zest
1 tbsp whole milk
4 apricots, halved
   and stoned
25g flaked almonds

YOU WILL NEED
9cm round cutter
12-hole muffin trays x 2

Apricot and Almond Tarts

The crisp pastry in these little tarts (made in muffin tins) is filled with almond frangipane and topped with sliced apricots. With no buttercream or chocolate involved, they are ideal for those occasions when eating with fingers could otherwise get messy.

1. Make the pastry. Tip the flour into a large mixing bowl, add the salt and butter. Using a round-bladed knife, cut the butter into the flour until the pieces are half their original size.

2. Using your fingertips, rub the butter into the flour until the mixture resembles fine breadcrumbs. Stir in the icing sugar and ground almonds and mix until combined.

3. Make a well in the centre. Add the egg and 1½ tablespoons of the milk and bring together to a smooth dough, adding the remaining milk if needed.

4. Turn out the dough onto the work surface, knead very lightly and briefly and flatten into a disc. Cover and chill for 1 hour, until firm.

5. Roll out the pastry on a lightly floured work surface until 2mm thick. Using the 9cm round cutter, cut out 18 discs, re-rolling the trimmings as necessary.

6. Carefully and neatly press one pastry disc into each muffin cup and spoon ½ teaspoon of the jam into each pastry case. Arrange the tins on a baking tray and chill the pastry while you prepare the filling. Heat the oven to 170°C/150°C fan/Gas 3.

7. Make the filling. Beat the butter and sugar in a stand mixer fitted with the beater, on medium speed for 3–5 minutes, until pale and creamy, scraping down the sides of the bowl from time to time.

8. Add the eggs and the egg yolk, a little at a time, beating well between each addition.

Continues overleaf

9. Sift the ground almonds, flour, baking powder and salt into the bowl, then add the lemon zest and milk and beat for another 1 minute, until smooth and thoroughly combined.

10. Carefully spoon the filling mixture into the pastry cases on top of the jam and level with the back of the spoon.

11. Cut each apricot half into 8 thin slices or wedges. Arrange 4 slices on top of each tart and scatter equally with the flaked almonds. Bake on the middle shelf for about 25 minutes, until the pastry is crisp and the filling risen and golden brown.

12. Leave the tarts to cool in the tins for about 4 minutes, then transfer to a wire rack to cool completely. Serve at room temperature, lightly dusted with icing sugar.

FOR THE CAKES

175g unsalted butter, softened
175g caster sugar
3 eggs, lightly beaten
150g plain flour
25g cornflour
2 tsp baking powder
1 tsp ground ginger
pinch of salt
50g ground almonds
finely grated zest of 2 unwaxed lemons
finely grated zest of 2 unwaxed limes
juice of ½ lemon
juice of 1 lime
2 balls stem ginger, drained and finely chopped
2 tbsp whole milk
25g flaked almonds

FOR THE DRIZZLE

juice of 1½ lemons
juice of 1 lime
1 tbsp stem ginger syrup
3 tbsp granulated sugar

YOU WILL NEED

8 mini loaf cases

Makes
8

Hands on
20 mins

Bake
25 mins

Lemon, Lime and Ginger Drizzle Cakes

These citrussy loaf cakes have a double hit of ginger, giving them a lovely, warming flavour. Mini loaf-cake cases are readily available in big supermarkets, cookware shops, and online, and make perfect individual cakes to give away or sell at a cake sale, or to pack as a treat in a picnic or lunchbox.

1. Heat the oven to 180°C/160°C fan/Gas 4 and arrange the mini loaf cases on a baking tray.

2. Make the cakes. Beat the butter and sugar in a stand mixer fitted with the beater, on medium speed for 3–5 minutes, until pale and creamy, scraping down the sides of the bowl with a rubber spatula from time to time.

3. Add the eggs, a little at a time, beating well between each addition.

4. Sift together the flour, cornflour, baking powder, ground ginger and salt into the bowl. Add the ground almonds, lemon zest, lime zest, lemon juice, lime juice, chopped ginger and milk, then beat on medium speed for 1 minute, until well combined.

5. Divide the mixture equally between the loaf cases, filling them two thirds full, and scatter with the flaked almonds. Bake on the middle shelf for 25 minutes, until golden brown, well risen and a skewer inserted into the centre of each cake comes out clean. Remove from the oven and transfer to a wire rack to cool slightly.

6. Meanwhile, make the drizzle. Mix the lemon juice, lime juice, stem ginger syrup and granulated sugar together in a jug, stirring until the sugar has nearly dissolved. Using a cocktail stick, poke 8 holes into each warm cake and slowly pour over the sugary syrup. Leave to cool completely before serving.

FOR THE SHORTBREAD
150g plain flour, sifted
75g unsalted butter,
    cubed and chilled
25g crunchy or smooth
    peanut butter
50g light muscovado sugar
175g salted roasted peanuts,
    roughly chopped

FOR THE CARAMEL
250g condensed milk
125g unsalted butter
100g caster sugar
50g golden syrup
1 tsp vanilla paste

FOR THE TOPPING
125g 70% dark chocolate,
    roughly chopped
75g milk chocolate,
    roughly chopped
25g unsalted butter, cubed
50g white chocolate,
    roughly chopped

YOU WILL NEED
20cm square traybake
    tin, greased, then lined
    (base and sides) with
    baking paper
small paper piping bag

Makes
16

Hands on
30 mins

Bake
18 mins

Peanut and Caramel Millionaire's Shortbread

Millionaire's shortbread is always a crowd-pleaser, but this recipe has an extra peanut twist. Store in an airtight container for up to one week – the caramel becomes even more fudgy over a few days.

1. Heat the oven to 180°C/160°C fan/Gas 4.

2. Make the shortbread base. Tip the flour into a bowl, rub in the cubed butter with your fingertips until only small flecks remain.

3. Add the peanut butter and sugar and mix again to combine and until the shortbread starts to clump. Tip into the prepared tin and press level using your hands, then firmly with the back of a spoon. Prick with a fork and bake for about 18 minutes, until pale golden brown. Leave to cool in the tin (the shortbread will firm as it cools).

4. Make the caramel. Tip all the ingredients into a medium, heavy-based pan and set over a low heat for 1–2 minutes, stirring to dissolve the sugar. Bring to the boil and cook, whisking continuously, for about 5 minutes, until reduced, thickened slightly and caramel-coloured.

5. Working quickly, remove the pan from the heat and spoon 2–3 tablespoons of caramel onto the shortbread, spreading it level. Scatter the peanuts over and carefully spoon over the remaining caramel in an even layer. Tap the tin sharply on the work surface to level out the contents. Leave to cool to room temperature to firm up.

6. Make the topping. Combine the chopped dark and milk chocolates with the butter in a heatproof bowl and set over a pan of barely simmering water to melt. Stir until smooth and remove from the heat. In a clean bowl, melt the white chocolate in the same way.

7. Spread the dark chocolate over the caramel. Spoon the white chocolate into a piping bag, twist the top and snip the end. Pipe lines on top of the dark chocolate, then draw a cocktail stick through them, up then down, to feather. Leave to set, then cut into 16 squares.

Makes
16

Hands on
45 mins

Bake
20 mins

plus rising

BAKER'S FAVOURITE

Sura's Parsley, Feta and Spinach Turkish Pastries

These Turkish pastries are my go-to when I'm pressed for time but want to make something delicious for a picnic, afternoon snack, or even a light dinner. They are especially good on-the-go because the filling is neatly encased in the bun. They freeze well, too – just reheat from frozen for 10 minutes in the oven.

FOR THE DOUGH
100ml whole milk
500g strong white
 bread flour
7g fast-action dried yeast
1 tsp salt
1 tbsp caster sugar
1 large egg
50ml olive oil
100ml lukewarm water

FOR THE FILLING
200g baby spinach
 leaves, washed
kettle of just-boiled water
15g flat-leaf parsley,
 finely chopped
200g feta cheese
grated zest of
 1 unwaxed lemon
¼ tsp ground cumin
freshly ground black pepper

YOU WILL NEED
2 proving bags

1. Gently warm the milk in a small pan over a low heat.

2. Place the flour in the bowl of a stand mixer fitted with the dough hook. Add the yeast, salt and sugar, then the egg, olive oil, lukewarm water and warm milk. Mix on a slow speed for 5 minutes, until the dough is smooth and elastic. Cover and leave to rise in a warm place for about 1–1½ hours, until doubled in size.

3. Meanwhile make the filling. Place the spinach in a colander in the sink. Pour the just-boiled water over the spinach until it wilts, then press out as much moisture as possible and pat dry with kitchen paper. Place on a chopping board and chop roughly, then transfer to a mixing bowl. Add the parsley and feta and break up with a fork. Add the lemon zest and cumin and season with a good grinding of pepper. Mix with a fork until roughly combined.

4. Turn out the risen dough onto a lightly dusted work surface and roll into a long, fat sausage. Cut into 16 equal portions (about 50g each). Shape each into a round about 10cm in diameter.

5. Place small, equal amounts of the filling in the centre of each round. Pull the dough up over the filling and pinch to seal (they'll be oval in shape), then flatten slightly. Place seam-side down, spaced well apart, on two baking trays. Place each tray in a proving bag and leave for about 1 hour, until risen and almost doubled in size.

6. Heat the oven to 200°C/180°C fan/Gas 6. Bake the pastries for about 20 minutes, until risen and golden brown. Serve warm or cold.

FOR THE CHOUX PASTRY
45g strong white bread flour
45g plain flour
5g caster sugar
65ml whole milk
55g unsalted butter
¼ tsp salt
2 large eggs

FOR THE CRÈME PÂTISSIÈRE
150ml whole milk
80ml double cream
65g caster sugar
4 large egg yolks
20g cornflour
40g unsalted butter

FOR THE SALTED CARAMEL
100g caster sugar
50g unsalted butter
70g double cream
1 tsp sea salt flakes
1 tsp vanilla extract

FOR THE CARAMELISED HAZELNUTS
3 blanched hazelnuts

FOR THE RASPBERRY PURÉE
150g raspberries
1 tsp caster sugar

FOR THE SALTED CARAMEL ICING
50–70g fondant icing sugar

FOR THE GLAZE
100g caster sugar
2 tsp gelatine powder
¼ tsp edible gold powder

TO DECORATE
cornflour, for dusting
50g ready-to-roll dark red fondant
30g freeze-dried raspberry powder
50g fondant icing sugar
white sprinkles
3 raspberry halves
edible gold leaf

See 'You Will Need' overleaf

Makes
6

Hands on
1½ hours

Bake
30 mins

Prue's Raspberry and Salted Caramel Éclairs

Prue's éclairs are sure to put you in the running for the top prize at the next charity bake off. The choux makes enough for ten éclairs – bake them all, then make up six and freeze the remainder, or make double the quantity of filling and generously fill them all.

1. Heat the oven to 190°C/170°C fan/Gas 5. Draw ten 12cm-long lines, equally spaced apart, on the underside of the sheet of baking paper lining your baking sheet.

2. Make the choux pastry. Sift both types of flour and the sugar onto a sheet of baking paper.

3. Put the milk, butter and salt into a saucepan with 65ml water and heat gently until the butter melts – don't let the water boil before the butter has melted. Then, quickly bring the mixture to the boil and tip in the flour and sugar mixture in one go. Remove from the heat and beat furiously with a wooden spoon.

4. Return the pan to a low heat and continue to beat the dough for 4–5 minutes, until it is glossy and cleanly leaves the sides of the pan. The dough should cook slightly and dry out. Tip the dough into the bowl of a stand mixer and leave to cool until just warm.

5. With the mixer on medium, add the eggs, one at a time, beating well between each addition until smooth and the batter reluctantly drops off a spoon. Spoon the mixture into the piping bag with the closed star nozzle and pipe ten 12cm lines, using the drawn lines as a guide.

6. Bake on the middle shelf for 25–30 minutes, opening the oven door halfway through to release the steam, until golden brown and crisp. Remove from the oven, prick the bases with a wooden skewer and cool on a wire rack. (Once cooled, you can freeze four of the buns.)

Continues overleaf

YOU WILL NEED
baking sheet lined
    with baking paper
large piping bag fitted with
    a large closed star nozzle
medium piping bag fitted
    with a large ribbon nozzle
2 medium piping bags, each
    fitted with a jam syringe
small piping bag fitted with
    a medium writing nozzle

7. Make the crème pâtissière. Bring the milk and cream to the boil in a pan, then remove from the heat.

8. Whisk the sugar, egg yolks and cornflour in a stand mixer fitted with the whisk on medium speed until combined. Pour a little of the hot milk mixture onto the egg mixture, whisking continuously. Whisk in the rest of the hot milk until well combined, then return to the pan. Cook the mixture over a gentle heat, stirring continuously, until it thickens to a thick custard consistency.

9. Remove from the heat and pass the mixture through a sieve into a clean bowl. Add the butter and stir until melted and thoroughly combined. Cover with cling film and set aside.

10. Start to make the salted caramel. Heat the sugar in a heavy-based pan over a medium heat, shaking the pan from time to time without stirring, until the sugar dissolves and turns a dark amber colour. Remove from the heat and leave to cool slightly.

11. Make the caramelised hazelnuts. Stick the end of a wooden skewer into the side of each hazelnut, taking care not to split the hazelnut. Place a heavy chopping board on the edge of a work surface and a sheet of baking paper on the floor beneath it. One at a time, gently dip the hazelnuts in the caramel until coated, then place the skewers under the chopping board overhanging the work surface and let the caramel drip off the hazelnut in a long strand (the baking paper will catch the drip). Leave to cool and set, then gently remove the skewer and trim the strands of caramel so that all three are the same length.

12. Return the caramel pan to a low heat and add the butter, stirring to combine. Add the cream and stir continuously to a dark, golden, thick sauce. Remove from the heat, stir in the salt and leave to cool.

13. Make the raspberry purée. Tip the raspberries and sugar into a small pan and crush with a potato masher. Cook over a medium heat for 3–5 minutes, until the raspberries release their juices and the liquid thickens. Remove from the heat and pass through a clean sieve into a bowl, scraping the purée from the underside of the sieve. Leave to cool.

14. Divide the crème pâtissière equally between 2 bowls, then fold the raspberry purée into one bowl until thoroughly combined. Cover the surface with baking paper to stop a skin forming and chill until required.

15. Fold 75g of the cooled salted caramel and the vanilla extract into the other bowl of crème pâtissière until thoroughly combined. Cover as before and chill until required.

16. Make the salted caramel icing. Mix the remaining salted caramel with the fondant icing sugar until stiff, smooth and glossy. Spoon into the medium piping bag fitted with a large ribbon nozzle. Set aside.

17. Make the glaze. Tip the sugar into a pan with 150ml water. Bring to the boil, then reduce the heat and simmer, without stirring, for 5 minutes, until syrupy. Remove from the heat and set aside. Pour 2 tablespoons of the syrup into a small bowl and reserve.

18. Sprinkle the gelatine over 100ml water in a small heatproof bowl and leave to stand for 2–3 minutes, until softened and swelled (bloomed). Set the bowl over a pan of gently simmering water, stirring occasionally until the gelatine dissolves. Remove from the heat and stir into the sugar syrup in the pan. Pour the mixture into a shallow bowl (at least the length of an éclair), then stir in the edible gold powder. Leave to cool and thicken slightly.

19. To assemble the éclairs, make 2 small holes in the base of each éclair with the tip of a small, sharp knife.

20. Spoon the raspberry crème pâtissière into the piping bag fitted with a jam syringe and pipe three of the éclairs full of raspberry filling.

21. Spoon the salted caramel crème pâtissière into the second piping bag fitted with a jam syringe and pipe three of the éclairs full of salted caramel filling.

22. Pipe the salted caramel icing neatly on top of the salted caramel-filled éclairs, then dip them into the gold glaze to coat the icing. (If the glaze has started to set before you dip the éclairs, simply warm it over a pan of gently simmering water.) Transfer to a wire rack to set. Once set, decorate each one with a caramelised hazelnut.

23. For the raspberry éclairs, on a surface lightly dusted with cornflour, roll out the red fondant to 1.5–2mm thick and cut three 12 x 2.5cm-wide strips. Trim the ends of each strip into a curve the same shape as the ends of the éclairs. Brush the raspberry éclairs with some of the reserved sugar syrup, then stick a fondant strip on top of each one. Tip the freeze-dried raspberry powder onto a plate. Brush the top of the fondant with the sugar syrup, then dip into the powder to coat.

24. Mix the 50g fondant icing sugar with enough water to make a stiff, pourable icing, then spoon into the piping bag fitted with a writing nozzle. Pipe 4 lines along the length of each raspberry éclair and decorate with white sprinkles. Finally, decorate with a halved raspberry topped with a little edible gold leaf.

FOR THE DATE PURÉE
180g pitted dried dates
150ml just-boiled water

FOR THE APPLE PURÉE
3 eating apples (such
    as Cox or Braeburn),
    peeled, cored and sliced

FOR THE CAKES
80ml light olive oil,
    plus extra for greasing
100g light brown soft sugar
120ml almond milk,
    plus extra for
    frosting (optional)
1 tsp vanilla paste
180g plain flour, sifted
1 tsp baking powder
1 tsp bicarbonate of soda

FOR THE CARAMEL SAUCE
50ml tinned full-fat
    coconut milk
75g light brown soft sugar
2 tsp golden syrup
¼ tsp vanilla paste
1 level tsp cornflour

FOR THE VANILLA FROSTING
200g icing sugar, sifted
60g vegan spread
½ tsp vanilla paste

TO DECORATE
24 edible flowers
    (preferably violas)
12 sprigs of micro-mint
    or mint tops

YOU WILL NEED
12-hole, loose-bottomed
    mini sandwich tin, oiled
medium paper piping bag

Makes 12

Hands on 45 mins

Bake 25 mins

Sticky Toffee Apple Cakes

Inspired by the rich, caramel flavour of the British toffee apple, these decadent and sticky mini cakes are jam-packed with dates and apples. Decorated with violas, or other dainty edible flowers, they look especially pretty on a cake stall or served from a tray at a tea party.

1. Make the date purée. Place the dates in a pan and cover with the just-boiled water. Bring to the boil, then reduce the heat and simmer for 10 minutes, until soft. Remove from the heat, leave to cool slightly, then blitz with a hand-held stick blender to a purée. Set aside.

2. Make the apple purée. Place the apples in a pan with 1 tablespoon of water. Cook over a low heat, gently simmering for 10 minutes, until soft. Remove from the heat, leave to cool slightly, then blitz with a hand-held stick blender to a purée. Weigh out 200g of the purée and set aside (freeze any leftovers for another time, if necessary).

3. Make the cakes. Heat the oven to 180°C/160°C fan/Gas 4.

4. Place the olive oil, sugar, almond milk and vanilla paste in a large mixing bowl and whisk with a balloon whisk until combined. Add the date purée and the 200g apple purée, then whisk for another 1 minute, until smooth.

5. Stir in the flour, baking powder and bicarbonate of soda and gently beat together to a thick batter. Do not over-mix. Divide the mixture equally between the oiled hollows in the tin.

6. Bake for 20–25 minutes, until well risen and golden brown with cracked tops, and a skewer inserted into the centres comes out clean. Leave to cool completely in the tin.

7. Make the caramel sauce. Place 1 tablespoon of the coconut milk in a small bowl and set aside, then place the remaining coconut milk in a small pan with the sugar, golden syrup and vanilla paste. Cook over a low heat, stirring, until the sugar dissolves.

Continues overleaf

8. Mix the cornflour into the reserved coconut milk to a creamy paste, then whisk this into the hot sauce. Bring to the boil, then reduce the heat and simmer for about 5 minutes, until the sauce thickens and reduces to a slightly thick syrup. Remove from the heat and leave to cool.

9. Make the frosting. Place the icing sugar, vegan spread and vanilla paste in a medium mixing bowl and mix with an electric hand whisk, adding a splash of almond milk if necessary, until light and creamy. Spoon into the piping bag and snip the end to make a hole.

10. Turn the cakes out of the tins and pipe a swirl of frosting onto each one. Pour or spoon over a little caramel sauce, then decorate with fresh flowers and micro mint leaves or mint tips.

100g Sourdough Starter
(see p.223)
350ml cool (blood-temperature) water
450g strong white bread flour, plus 1 tbsp
50g spelt, wholemeal or rye flour
10g sea salt flakes, ground
1 tbsp rice flour

YOU WILL NEED
dough scraper
1kg banneton or a medium mixing bowl, lined with a clean, dry tea towel
large plastic bag or plastic shower cap
Dutch oven/cast-iron casserole, or baking stone
lame (optional)

Makes
1kg loaf

Hands on
30 mins

Bake
40 mins

plus rising

Sourdough

Use good-quality organic flour for the best sourdough, and a Dutch oven or cast-iron casserole, which give the bread a deep-brown, crisp crust. Make sure your starter (see page 223) is active before you begin – remember that the timings are weather-dependent: activating the starter and rising takes longer when it's cooler. Then, make yummy sandwiches (or just slather in butter!) for all to enjoy.

1. For this recipe your starter needs to be at its active peak and ready to use first thing in the morning. Feed the starter at around 10pm, ready to mix your dough about 8am the next morning. The starter should have doubled in size and be full of air bubbles before you start (drop ½ teaspoon of starter into a small bowl of warm water – it if floats, it's ready; if it sinks it needs a little more time, or you may need to feed it again and wait another 6–8 hours at room temperature).

2. Spoon the starter into a large mixing bowl, preferably glass so that you can see the bubbles forming in the dough. Add the cool water (blood temperature or a little warmer) and mix until combined.

3. Add the white flour and the spelt, wholemeal or rye flour and, using one hand, mix for about 2 minutes, until combined. There should be no dry flour patches, but the dough will not be smooth. Cover loosely with a damp tea towel and set aside for 30 minutes in a warm, draught-free area of the kitchen, until softer and less lumpy.

4. Add the ground salt to the dough with 1 tablespoon of water and, using one hand, mix until combined, twisting and squelching the dough between your fingers. Continue mixing for about 1 minute, until smooth and the salt and water are thoroughly mixed in. Cover and leave for another 30 minutes, until lighter and more elastic.

5. Using a wet hand, pick up the top edge of the dough. Stretch it out and fold it over to meet the bottom edge. Turn the bowl through 90° clockwise and stretch and fold again. Repeat a further three times, turning the bowl after each fold. Cover and rest for 30 minutes.

Continues on page 222

6. Repeat the stretching and folding another three times – each set 30 minutes apart. You'll do four sets of folds in total over a 2-hour period.

7. Cover the bowl and set aside for 2 hours, until the dough has increased by at least one third and air bubbles appear on the top and sides. If not, cover and leave for another 30–45 minutes, then check again.

8. Very lightly dust the work surface with flour and, using a dough scraper, Turn out the dough. Using the scraper or lightly floured hands, form the dough into a smooth, tight ball, cupping the dough from the bottom and swiftly turning it anticlockwise in as few moves as possible. Cover with the upturned bowl and leave for another 20 minutes.

9. Meanwhile, mix the rice flour with the extra 1 tablespoon of white flour and dust the banneton or cloth-lined bowl with the mixture.

10. Lightly dust the top of the dough with white flour and, using the dough scraper, flip the ball over so that the floured side is on the work surface. Lightly stretch out the edges of the dough. Picture the dough as a clock face: starting at 12 o'clock pull the outside edge of the dough into the middle, make a 90° turn and repeat 5–6 times until you have brought all the edges into the middle and the dough starts to form a ball. Turn the ball over, smooth-side up, then cup your hands around the dough and gently pull it towards you on the work surface to tighten the bottom. Using the dough scraper, quickly but gently flip the dough over onto one hand and carefully lower it into the prepared banneton or bowl, rounded, smooth-side down. Cover with a bag or shower cap and leave to rest for 30–45 minutes, then transfer to the fridge to slowly prove overnight.

11. When you're ready to bake, heat the oven to 240°C/220°C fan/Gas 9 (or as hot as your oven will go). Place a Dutch oven or cast-iron casserole or baking stone in the oven to heat up for 45 minutes.

12. Remove the bag or shower cap from the bread and lay a piece of baking paper on top of the banneton or bowl. Place a baking sheet on top and very gently flip out the bread onto the paper. Using a lame or very sharp knife, cut a slash across the dough about 1cm deep and at a 45° angle. Carefully remove the very hot pan from the oven and remove the lid. Gently lift the dough on the baking paper and lower it into the pan. Cover with the lid and bake for 30 minutes until the bread has risen dramatically and started to turn golden.

13. Remove the lid from the pan and cook for a further 10 minutes, or until the bread is a deep golden brown with a very crisp crust. Remove the bread from the pan and leave to cool on a wire rack before slicing.

SOURDOUGH STARTER

Making a starter can take anything from 6 days to 2 weeks, depending on which flour you use and the ambient temperature of your kitchen.

YOU WILL NEED
about 150g organic strong white bread flour
about 150g organic spelt or rye flour
lukewarm water (tap is okay, but it must
   not be too warm or cold)
large lidded jar

Day One
Combine the white and spelt or rye flour and store in an airtight box or jar. Mix 25g of the flour mixture with 25ml cool water in a glass or ceramic bowl and beat to a smooth paste. Cover the bowl loosely with baking paper, securing it with a rubber band, and leave for 24 hours at room temperature. Total weight = 50g.

Day Two
Mix 25g of the flour mixture with 25ml lukewarm water to a smooth paste and add to the Day One starter. Beat well to combine, then cover again and set aside for 24 hours. Total weight = 100g.

Day Three
Remove half the mixture (50g) and discard. Add a further 25g of the flour mixture and 25ml lukewarm water to the remaining starter. Beat to combine, then scoop into a lidded glass, or ceramic or stoneware jar. Cover loosely with the lid and set aside for 24 hours. Total weight = 100g.

Day Four
Repeat day three. Total weight = 100g.

Day Five
Mix 100g of the flour mixture and 100ml lukewarm water to a smooth paste and add to the starter. Beat well to combine, then cover loosely with the lid and leave for 24 hours. Total weight = 300g.

Day Six
Remove half the starter (150g) and add 75g of the flour mixture and 75ml water. Total weight = 300g.

By now your starter should be bubbly and active and have a fresh, yeasty smell. You can repeat this process for another 6 days, removing half the starter and adding the same amount of water and flour mixture each day. Remember to keep the ratio of flour to water the same at every feed. If the starter is slow to get started after 6 days, feed it twice a day, each feed 12 hours apart.

Once active, store your starter in the fridge between use – unless you bake every day or every other day, in which case store at cool room temperature. If you store it in the fridge, bring the starter back to room temperature and feed the day before using.

FOR THE BISCUIT BASE
250g caramelised biscuits
85g unsalted butter, melted

FOR THE CHEESECAKE LAYER
600g full-fat cream cheese
125g caster sugar
3 tbsp speculoos
   or caramelised
   biscuit spread
3 eggs
150ml soured cream
2 tsp instant espresso
   powder dissolved in
   1 tsp just-boiled water
1 tbsp cornflour

FOR THE SWIRL TOPPING
2 tbsp speculoos
   or caramelised
   biscuit spread
1 tbsp soured cream

YOU WILL NEED
20 x 30cm baking tin,
   greased, then lined
   (base and sides)
   with baking paper
small piping bag fitted with
   a medium plain nozzle

Makes 15

Hands on 30 mins *plus chilling*

Bake 35 mins

Speculoos Cheesecake Squares

The biscuit base of this cheesecake is made from lightly spiced, caramelised Belgian biscuits called speculoos, while the filling and topping uses speculoos biscuit spread (available in jars) to give an irresistible caramel flavour. Serve in squares or fingers.

1. Heat the oven to 180°C/160°C fan/Gas 4.

2. Make the biscuit base. Crush the biscuits into fine crumbs either in a food processor using the pulse button or in a freezer bag with a rolling pin. Tip into a bowl, add the melted butter and combine.

3. Tip the buttery crumbs into the lined tin, spread level and, using the flat base of a glass or mug, press into a firm layer. Bake for 5 minutes, until starting to firm up and turn crisp. Leave to cool. Reduce the oven temperature to 170°C/150°C fan/Gas 3.

4. Make the cheesecake layer. In a large mixing bowl, beat the cream cheese until smooth. Add the caster sugar and speculoos or caramelised biscuit spread and mix again for 1 minute. Add the eggs, one at a time, beating well between each addition, then add the soured cream, espresso and cornflour and beat again until smooth.

5. Reserve 2 tablespoons of the cheesecake mixture and spoon the remainder into the tin. Level with a palette knife.

6. Make the swirl topping. Combine the biscuit spread and soured cream with the reserved cheesecake mixture until smooth. Spoon the mixture into the piping bag and pipe over the top of the cheesecake in a random swirl. Using a round bladed knife, lightly marble the mixtures together, then tap the tin on the work surface to level.

7. Bake on the middle shelf for 30 minutes, until the cheesecake has set. Leave to cool to room temperature, then chill for at least 2 hours, until firm. Cut into squares or fingers. Cover and store in the fridge until ready to serve.

300g plain flour
3 tsp baking powder
1 tsp English mustard
    powder
½ tsp smoked paprika
pinch of salt
50g unsalted butter,
    cubed and chilled
125g mature Cheddar
    cheese, grated
25g Parmesan cheese,
    finely grated
4 spring onions, trimmed
    and finely sliced
100ml whole milk, plus
    1 tbsp for brushing
freshly ground black pepper

YOU WILL NEED
baking sheet, greased, then
    lined with baking paper
6cm round cutter

Makes
10–12

Hands on
20 mins

Bake
15 mins

Cheese and Spring Onion Scones

Savoury scones make a good option for a cake sale among all the sweet fairy cakes, buttercream and sprinkles. Although they're best eaten on the day of baking, the scones reheat beautifully. They are delicious with a bowl of tomato soup, or simply spread with butter as a snack.

1. Heat the oven to 200°C/180°C fan/Gas 6.

2. Sift the flour, baking powder, mustard powder and smoked paprika into a large mixing bowl. Season well with pepper, then add the salt and butter.

3. Using your fingertips, rub the butter into the dry ingredients until only small flecks are visible. Reserve 1 tablespoon of the Cheddar, then add the remainder to the bowl, along with the Parmesan and the spring onions and mix to combine.

4. Make a well in the centre and pour in the milk and 100ml water. Using a palette or round-bladed knife, mix until the dough is just combined. Turn out onto a lightly floured work surface and very lightly knead the dough for 10 seconds, until combined.

5. Flatten the dough into a disc, about 2–3cm thick. Dip the cutter into plain flour to prevent it sticking and stamp out as many rounds as you can. Place the rounds on the lined baking sheet, leaving a little space between each scone to allow for spreading during baking. Gather the trimmings, flatten out and stamp out more scones to give 10–12 in total.

6. Brush the top of each scone with a little milk and scatter evenly with the reserved Cheddar. Bake on the middle shelf for 13–15 minutes, until well-risen and golden brown. Remove from the oven and leave to cool on a wire rack.

CHAPTER SIX

Gatherings

Recipes

FOR THE DOUGH
110g unsalted butter
250g plain flour
1 tsp salt
3 egg yolks

FOR THE FLOURED BUTTER
375g unsalted butter,
   softened
150g plain flour

FOR THE FILLING
360g spinach, washed
kettle of just-boiled water
25g unsalted butter
1 tbsp lemon juice,
   plus an extra squeeze
   for the salmon
pinch of ground nutmeg
250g smoked salmon,
   roughly chopped
2 tsp horseradish sauce
freshly ground black pepper

FOR THE BACON CRUMB
olive oil, for frying
20g Parma ham

FOR THE QUAIL'S EGGS
50ml white wine vinegar
12 quail's eggs, chilled
celery salt, to garnish

YOU WILL NEED
10cm and 6cm fluted
   cutters
2 baking sheets,
   1 greased, then lined
   with baking paper

Makes
12

Hands on
1 ½ hours
plus chilling

Bake
30 mins

BAKER'S FAVOURITE

Rowan's Salmon and Horseradish Vol au Vents

This recipe came about almost by chance. After a busy morning's baking we needed something quick for lunch. Rummaging in the fridge produced eggs, spinach, smoked salmon and bacon. Laced with lemon and horseradish and piled on freshly baked crumpets, it was an instant hit. Serving the mixture in buttery puff pastry is even better. These are our go-to party food or light starter.

1. Make the dough. Melt the butter in a small pan over a low heat, then pour into a bowl and cool for 10 minutes. Place the flour in a separate bowl and stir in the melted butter, 100ml water, the salt and 2 of the egg yolks. Stir to form a soft ball of dough. Flatten into an 18cm square, wrap and chill for 2 hours.

2. Make the floured butter. Place the softened butter in a mixing bowl and beat in the flour with a wooden spoon until well blended. Flatten into a 36 x 18cm rectangle, wrap and chill for 2 hours.

3. Place the chilled butter on a lightly floured work surface. Place the square of dough on top, in the middle of the rectangle. Fold both ends of the butter over the dough to enclose it. Turn the dough by 90° and roll out again to a 36 x 18cm rectangle. Fold into 3 layers as before, then wrap and chill for at least 1 hour. Repeat the rolling, folding and chilling twice more, wrapping and chilling the final dough for 2 hours.

4. Cut the dough in half, then on a lightly floured work surface, roll out one half to a rectangle about 45 x 35cm (3–4mm thick). Using the 10cm cutter, cut out 12 discs. Place on the lined baking sheet and chill.

5. Roll out the remaining dough half and cut out another twelve 10cm discs. Using the 6cm cutter, cut out the middle of each disc to form 12 dough rings. Chill for 15 minutes.

Continues overleaf

6. Beat the remaining egg yolk with 1 teaspoon of water. Remove the pastry discs and rings from the fridge and, using a pastry brush, use the egg mixture to paint the tops of the discs. Place a pastry ring on top of each disc and brush the tops of the rings, taking care not to drip the egg-yolk mixture down the sides (which can prevent a good rise). Chill the vol au vents on the lined baking sheet for 1–2 hours.

7. Heat the oven to 190°C/170°C fan/Gas 5.

8. Place the vol au vents on the baking sheet on the middle shelf and put the second baking sheet on the top shelf (this helps to create an even rise). Bake for 25–30 minutes, until golden brown and well risen. Remove from the oven and leave to cool on the baking sheet. Using a small, pointed knife, cut out a circle of pastry in the middle of each vol au vent to make a lid, and set aside.

9. Meanwhile, make the filling. Place the spinach in a colander in the sink and pour over the kettle of just-boiled water, leaving it to drain well. Leave to cool, then squeeze out as much water as possible from the spinach. Melt the butter in a large pan, add the spinach, lemon juice and nutmeg and mix well. Set aside to cool.

10. Mix the salmon with the horseradish sauce, an extra squeeze of lemon juice and season with pepper.

11. Make the bacon crumb. Lightly oil a frying pan and heat to medium–hot. Add the Parma ham and fry for about 2–4 minutes, using a fish slice to press it down, until well browned. Remove from the pan, drain on kitchen paper, and leave to cool and crisp up further. Then, chop into crumbs.

12. For the quail's eggs, bring 500ml water to a simmer in a medium pan, then pour in the vinegar. Crack the eggs, one at a time, into the simmering water, then turn the heat down to its lowest setting. Poach for about 1 minute, until the whites are just set, then remove the eggs from the pan with a slotted spoon and drain. Use immediately, or chill the eggs in iced water until needed.

13. To assemble the vol au vents, divide the smoked salmon filling between the pastry cases, then top with a layer of spinach and press down. Top with a poached quail's eggs, sprinkle with Parma ham crumbs and a pinch of celery salt. Place the pastry lids on top and serve within 1 hour.

FOR THE PUFF PASTRY

250g unsalted butter, chilled
150g plain flour
100g strong white
  bread flour
pinch of salt
1 tsp white wine vinegar
  or lemon juice
125ml ice-cold water,
  plus extra if needed
1 tbsp whole milk,
  for brushing
1–2 tsp za'atar or sesame
  seeds, to finish

FOR THE FILLING

3 tbsp olive oil
1 onion, sliced
1 fennel bulb, trimmed,
  halved and thinly sliced
2 fat garlic cloves,
  finely chopped
½ tsp dried chilli flakes
250g baby spinach leaves
1 large courgette, trimmed
  and coarsely grated
1 rounded tbsp chopped
  flat-leaf parsley
1 rounded tbsp chopped dill
1 tsp finely grated zest
  of unwaxed lemon
200g feta
1 egg, beaten
salt and freshly ground
  black pepper

YOU WILL NEED

28cm dinner plate
2 baking sheets,
  1 greased, then lined
  with baking paper
32cm serving plate

Serves 4-6

Hands on 1 hour plus chilling

Bake 40 mins

Spinach, Fennel and Feta Galette

This is a delicious option for a vegetarian gathering. Try to make the puff at least 3 hours ahead (even the day before) to give it plenty of time to rest. You can prepare the filling in advance, too.

1. Make the pastry. Cube 50g of the chilled butter. Combine both types of flour and the salt in a mixing bowl. Using your fingertips, rub in the cubed butter until incorporated. Make a well in the middle, add the vinegar or lemon juice and ice-cold water and mix with a palette knife to bring together, adding a little more water, if needed. Flatten into a neat square, cover and chill with the remaining butter for 1 hour.

2. Lightly flour the work surface with plain flour and roll out the dough into a 45 x 15cm rectangle, with one of the short sides closest to you. Place the remaining 200g chilled butter between two sheets of baking paper and, using a rolling pin, flatten it into a neat 13cm square (slightly smaller than one third of the pastry rectangle).

3. Place the butter on the middle third of the pastry rectangle and fold the bottom third of pastry over it, brushing off any excess flour, then fold the top third down, as if folding a business letter, to completely encase the butter.

4. Flour the work surface and rolling pin. Turn the pastry through 90° clockwise and, using a short, sharp, tapping–rolling action, roll out the pastry into a neat rectangle as before. Fold the bottom third of the rectangle over the middle third and the top third down, brushing off any excess flour. Turn the pastry through 90° clockwise, wrap and chill for 1 hour (keeping the pastry flat and in the same position).

5. Lightly flour the work surface and roll out the pastry again as before, keeping the sides and ends as neat as possible. Fold the pastry as before, turn through 90° clockwise, then wrap and chill for another 1 hour (keeping the pastry flat and in the same position).

Continues overleaf

6. Repeat this rolling, folding and chilling twice more. After the final chilling, roll out the dough – you will have rolled the pastry 6 times in total. (Keep a note of the number of rolls, folds and chills, as it's easy to lose track.) Cover and chill for at least 2 hours before using.

7. While the pastry is chilling, make the filling. Heat the oil in a large sauté pan, add the onion and cook over a low–medium heat, stirring often, for about 5 minutes, until softened.

8. Add the fennel, garlic and chilli flakes and cook, stirring often, for 8–10 minutes, until the fennel is tender.

9. In a steamer, steam the spinach until just wilted, then drain and squeeze out any excess moisture. Add to the pan along with the courgette, then increase the heat slightly and cook for another 3 minutes to soften the courgette and cook off any excess moisture. Remove from the heat, tip into a large bowl, add the chopped herbs and lemon zest and leave to cool to room temperature.

10. Crumble the feta into the bowl, add the beaten egg, season well with salt and pepper and mix gently to combine.

11. Lightly flour the work surface and cut the pastry into 2 pieces, one slightly larger than the other. Using a 28cm dinner plate as a guide, roll out the smaller piece to about 2–3mm thick, and cut out a large pastry disc. Place it on the lined baking sheet.

12. Spoon the cooled filling neatly into the middle of the disc, leaving a 2cm border, and brush the border with water.

13. Using a 32cm serving plate as a guide, roll out the remaining pastry and cut out a second pastry disc. Carefully place the second disc on top of the filling, using your hands to gently smooth it over. Press the pastry edges together to seal.

14. Using a small, sharp knife 'knock up' the edges of the pie to seal, then chill for 20 minutes. While the pie is chilling, heat the oven to 180°C/160°C fan/Gas 4 and place a large, heavy-based baking sheet on the middle shelf to heat up.

15. Brush the top of the pie with milk and, using the tip of a knife, cut a pattern into but not through the pastry. Cut a small cross in the middle for steam to escape and sprinkle with za'atar or sesame seeds.

16. Slide the baking sheet into the oven on top of the hot baking sheet. Bake for 35–40 minutes, until the pastry is puffed up, golden and crisp, and the filling is piping hot. Cool for 2 minutes, then serve in wedges.

FOR THE PASTRY

FOR THE PASTRY
250g plain flour
½ tsp salt
125g unsalted butter
25g finely grated Parmesan
2–3 tbsp cold water

FOR THE FILLING
2 eggs
200ml double cream
50g grated mozzarella
   and Cheddar mixture
2 tbsp 'nduja paste
1 roasted red pepper from
   a jar, well drained and
   sliced into thin strips
12 jalapeño pepper slices
   from a jar
2 thin salami sticks
   (22g each), thinly sliced
6 mini mozzarella
   balls, drained
a few micro basil leaves,
   to garnish

YOU WILL NEED
10cm individual quiche
   tins (3cm deep) x 6
baking beans

Makes
6

Hands on
45 mins

Bake
30 mins

Hot 'n' Spicy Quiches

'Nduja, a spicy Calabrian salami paste, gives a rich flavour to these quiches, filled with cheese, peppers and salami to create the perfect pizza-flavour combo wrapped in crisp pastry. They are delicious served as a light lunch with salad alongside.

1. Heat the oven to 220°C/200°C fan/Gas 7. Place the flour, salt, butter and Parmesan in a food processor and blitz to fine crumbs.

2. Add the water and blitz for a few more seconds to a rough dough. Turn out the dough onto the work surface and use your hands to bring it together into a ball. Flatten slightly, then wrap and chill for 15 minutes.

3. Dust the work surface with flour. Divide the pastry into 6 equal pieces and roll each out to a 16cm circle. Press 1 pastry circle into the base and up the sides of each quiche tin, and trim the edges. Line each pastry case with a scrunched-up circle of baking paper and fill with baking beans.

4. Place the pastry cases on a baking tray and blind bake for 15 minutes, then remove from the oven and turn the temperature down to 180°C/160°C fan/Gas 4. Remove the paper and beans.

5. While the pastry cases are baking, make the filling. Beat the eggs and cream together and stir in half the grated cheese mixture.

6. Spread 1 level teaspoon of 'nduja in the base of each part-baked pastry case. Divide the egg mixture equally between the pastry cases. Add the sliced red pepper, dividing the slices equally between the quiches, and add 2 slices of jalapeño per quiche. Top with slices of salami. Break each mozzarella ball into 3 pieces and place the thirds into the quiches, then sprinkle with the remaining grated cheese.

7. Bake the quiches for 15 minutes, until just set. Allow to cool, then serve at room temperature, topped with basil leaves.

1 large garlic bulb,
   unpeeled
1 tbsp olive oil
350g strong white
   bread flour
175g plain flour
7g fast-action dried yeast
½ tsp caster sugar
1 tsp salt
275ml whole milk,
   plus 1 tbsp for glazing
1 tbsp malt extract
1 egg, lightly beaten,
   plus 1 yolk, for glazing
50g unsalted butter,
   softened
2 tbsp finely chopped
   flat-leaf parsley
1 tbsp chopped dill
2 tbsp extra-virgin olive oil

YOU WILL NEED
30 x 20cm baking tray,
   greased, then lined
   (base and sides)
   with baking paper

Makes
12

Hands on
30 mins
plus rising

Bake
25 minutes

Herby Garlic Rolls

A tray of warm, golden bread rolls drenched in a herby olive oil is hard to resist. These rolls have a tender crumb and gentle garlic flavour, and are perfect served at a gathering as a starter with a bowl of soup, or as part of a spread. You could make smaller rolls, but remember to reduce the rising and baking times accordingly.

1. Heat the oven to 180°C/160°C fan/Gas 4.

2. Place the whole, unpeeled bulb of garlic in a piece of foil, drizzle with the olive oil and wrap up tightly. Place in a small baking tray or roasting tin and roast for 35–40 minutes, until the cloves are tender. Leave the garlic to cool and turn off the oven.

3. Meanwhile, mix together both types of flour, along with the yeast, sugar and salt in a stand mixer fitted with a dough hook.

4. Gently warm the milk either in a small pan over a low heat or in a microwave. Stir in the malt extract until combined.

5. Pour the milk mixture into the mixer bowl with the beaten whole egg and butter. Mix until combined, then knead, on low–medium speed for 4–5 minutes, until smooth and elastic (the dough will be slightly sticky, so it is easier to mix in a stand mixer than by hand).

6. Squeeze the soft, cooled garlic cloves from the skins and mash to a smooth purée. Add the purée to the dough and knead briefly to combine.

7. Shape the dough into a ball and place in a lightly oiled bowl. Cover loosely with a slightly damp tea towel and leave to rise for about 1 hour, or until doubled in size.

8. Turn out the dough onto a lightly floured work surface. Knead gently for 30 seconds to knock out any large air pockets, then shape into a disc. Cover with an upturned bowl and leave to rest for another 10 minutes.

Continues overleaf

9. Divide the dough equally into 12 portions, then shape into neat balls with the seams on the undersides.

10. Arrange the dough balls neatly in the lined baking tray – they should be just touching, not squashed together. Cover loosely and leave to prove for 1 hour, until light, puffy and almost doubled in size.

11. Heat the oven to 180°C/160°C fan/Gas 4.

12. Mix the egg yolk with the extra 1 tablespoon of milk and carefully brush over the top of each roll. Bake on the middle shelf for 20–25 minutes, until well-risen and golden brown.

13. While the rolls are baking, mix together the chopped parsley, dill and extra-virgin olive oil in a small bowl.

14. As soon as the rolls come out of the oven brush them generously with the herb oil. Leave to cool slightly before serving warm or at room temperature.

FOR THE SPONGE
3 large eggs
75g caster sugar
50g gluten-free
   self-raising flour
30g cocoa powder

FOR THE MOUSSE
4 platinum-grade
   gelatine leaves
100ml pomegranate juice
300g frozen mixed red
   berries, defrosted;
   or fresh strawberries
   and raspberries
3 large eggs, separated
225g caster sugar
200ml double cream

FOR THE JELLY TOPPING
2½ platinum-grade
   gelatine leaves
100g caster sugar
75ml grenadine
50g pomegranate seeds

TO DECORATE
12 raspberries
20g pistachios
15g pomegranate seeds

YOU WILL NEED
33 x 23cm Swiss roll tin,
   greased, then lined
   (base and sides)
   with baking paper
sugar thermometer
20cm springform tin,
   greased, then lined
   (base and sides) with
   baking paper cut to
   come 2cm higher than
   the sides of the tin
kitchen blowtorch

Gluten Free

Serves
12

Hands on
2 hours

Bake
12 mins

plus chilling

BAKER'S FAVOURITE

Peter's Red Berry Delice

I first made this dessert when I was 15 for a dinner party with family friends. It was one of the first bakes I made that really wowed the table and has become a classic to bring out any time we want to feel a little fancy or show off a bit!

1. Heat the oven to 200°C/180°C fan/Gas 6.

2. Make the sponge. Whisk the eggs and sugar in a stand mixer fitted with the whisk, on high speed for about 8 minutes, until thick, fluffy and mousse-like, and the mixture leaves a ribbon trail when you lift the whisk.

3. Sift the flour and cocoa powder into the bowl and fold in with a large metal spoon. Spread out the mixture in the lined Swiss roll tin, right into the corners. Bake for 10–12 minutes, until the sponge is risen and springs back when pressed. Cool in the tin for 10 minutes, then turn out onto baking paper and remove the backing. Cool completely.

4. Make the mousse. Soak the gelatine leaves in 50ml water. Place the pomegranate juice and defrosted or fresh berries in a liquidiser or food processor and blend until smooth, then pass the mixture through a sieve into a jug (discard the contents of the sieve). Pour 225ml of the juice into a pan and heat until hot, but not boiling.

5. Meanwhile, using a balloon whisk, whisk the egg yolks with 85g of the sugar in a mixing bowl until pale. Gradually whisk in the hot berry juice, then return the mixture to the pan and cook over a low–medium heat, stirring continuously until the custard thickens and lightly coats the back of a spoon. Do not let the mixture boil.

Continues overleaf

6. Take the custard off the heat. Squeeze out any liquid from the soaked gelatine and stir the leaves into the custard until melted. Pass through a fine sieve into a clean bowl, cover the surface with cling film to prevent a skin forming and leave at room temperature to cool.

7. Place the egg whites and 30g of the sugar in the cleaned bowl of the stand mixer fitted with the whisk. Leave the mixture ready to go while you make a syrup for the mousse.

8. Gently heat the remaining 110g caster sugar in a saucepan with 35ml water until the sugar dissolves. Bring to the boil, without stirring, until it reaches 112°C on a sugar thermometer.

9. When the temperature reaches 107°C, start whisking the egg whites and sugar in the stand mixer on high speed until they form stiff peaks. Then, once the sugar syrup reaches 112°C, slowly pour the hot syrup into the egg whites, whisking continuously on high speed until the mixture cools to a thick, glossy meringue.

10. In a separate bowl, whisk the cream to soft peaks and gently fold the cream into the cooled meringue, then fold in the cooled berry custard.

11. To assemble, using the base of the springform tin as a template, cut out a circle of the sponge. Place the sponge inside the lined cake tin on a serving plate. Pour the mousse mixture into the tin, then chill for at least 4 hours, until set.

12. Make the jelly topping. Soak the gelatine leaves in a little cold water. Heat the sugar and 100ml water in a pan over a low-medium heat and bring to a simmer, stirring until the sugar dissolves. Remove from the heat, measure out 100ml of the syrup and combine this with the grenadine.

13. Squeeze any excess water from the gelatine and stir it into the hot syrup and grenadine mixture until dissolved. Leave to cool to room temperature. Once the jelly has cooled, add the pomegranate seeds and stir through.

14. Take the mousse cake out of the fridge and gently pour the jelly topping over, ensuring the mousse is evenly covered and the pomegranate seeds are evenly distributed throughout. Chill for about 30 minutes, until set.

15. To serve, remove the delice from the fridge. Remove the sides of the tin and peel away the baking paper. Arrange raspberries, pistachios and pomegranate seeds around the edge to decorate.

100g raisins
3 tbsp Pedro Ximenez
or other sweet sherry
700g full-fat cream cheese
225g caster sugar
1 tsp vanilla extract
½ tsp finely grated
unwaxed orange zest
½ tsp salt
5 eggs
275ml double cream
2 tsp plain flour, sifted

YOU WILL NEED
23cm springform tin,
greased, then lined
(based and sides) with
baking paper that comes
3–4cm higher than the
sides of the tin

Serves
10

Hands on
15 mins

Bake
45 mins

plus soaking

Basque Cheesecake

*This rich, decadent cheesecake originated in San Sebastian,
in Spain's Basque Country. Unlike New York-style cheesecake,
it is crustless and cooked on a high heat to caramelise the outside.
In this version, although not authentic, the sherry-soaked raisins,
along with the vanilla and orange zest help to balance out the
richness of the creamy interior. Bake it on the day you intend
to serve it to your gathered guests.*

1. Soak the raisins in the sherry for at least 4 hours, or preferably overnight, until plump and all of the sherry has been absorbed.

2. Heat the oven to 220°C/200°C fan/Gas 7.

3. Beat the cream cheese in a stand mixer fitted with the beater, on medium speed for 1–2 minutes, until light and creamy. Add the sugar, vanilla, orange zest and salt and mix again to combine.

4. Add the eggs, one at a time, beating well between each addition, then mix in the cream until thoroughly combined. Finally add the flour and mix again until smooth.

5. Fold the raisins and any remaining sherry into the mixture and pour into the lined tin.

6. Place the tin on a baking sheet and bake on the middle shelf for 45 minutes, until the cheesecake is puffed up, set with a firm wobble, and the outside is baked to a deep, dark caramel colour. Leave to cool in the tin.

7. Serve the cheesecake at room temperature or lightly chilled, but not cold, on the day of making. (It will firm up more the longer it is chilled.)

FOR THE WHISKED SPONGE
75g unsalted butter
8 eggs
200g caster sugar
200g plain flour
1½ tsp baking powder
pinch of salt
50g ground almonds

FOR THE COFFEE SYRUP
150ml freshly brewed hot
    espresso or strong coffee
1 tbsp demerara sugar

FOR THE MASCARPONE FILLING
6 egg yolks
75g caster sugar
4 tbsp Marsala or amaretto
pinch of salt
125g white chocolate,
    chopped
750g mascarpone cheese
150g 70% dark chocolate,
    coarsely grated

TO DECORATE
300ml double cream
1 tbsp chocolate-coated
    coffee beans, roughly
    chopped
cocoa powder, for dusting

YOU WILL NEED
20cm cake tins x 3, greased,
    then base-lined with
    baking paper and lightly
    dusted with flour
20cm, deep-sided
    springform tin
piping bag fitted with a
    medium plain nozzle

Serves
10

Hands on
1 ½ hours

Bake
20 mins

plus chilling

Tiramisù Cake

This towering cake is an elegant version of the much-loved, classic Italian dessert. Thin layers of light sponge are soaked in coffee and sandwiched together with a decadent mascarpone filling and a hint of dark chocolate. For the best results, bake the cake the day before you plan to assemble – the sponges are easier to slice in half. Assemble and chill the cake a good few hours before serving to allow the flavours to mingle.

1. Heat the oven to 180°C/160°C fan/Gas 4.

2. Make the sponge (the day before serving, ideally). Melt the butter and leave to cool slightly.

3. Whisk the eggs in a stand mixer fitted with the whisk. Add the sugar and whisk on medium speed for 5–7 minutes until thick and mousse-like, and the mixture leaves a ribbon trail when you lift the whisk.

4. Sift together the plain flour, baking powder and salt into the bowl, add the ground almonds and, using a large metal spoon, gently fold the dry ingredients into the wet.

5. Pour the melted butter around the inside edge of the bowl and gently fold in. Divide the mixture equally between the lined tins and level with a palette knife. Bake on the middle shelves for about 20 minutes, until golden, well risen and a skewer inserted into the centres comes out clean.

6. Leave the cakes to cool in the tins for 2 minutes, then turn out onto a wire rack to cool completely.

7. Make the coffee syrup. Pour the hot coffee into a bowl, add the sugar and stir until dissolved. Leave to cool.

8. Make the mascarpone filling. Whisk the egg yolks, sugar, Marsala or amaretto and salt in a heatproof bowl until fully combined.

Continues overleaf

9. Set the bowl over a pan of simmering water and continue whisking for about 5 minutes, until the mixture is hot to the touch, very thick and tripled in volume. Remove from the heat and plunge the bottom of the bowl into a sink of cold water to stop the cooking process, and whisk occasionally until cold.

10. Melt the white chocolate in a separate heatproof bowl set over a pan of barely simmering water. Stir until smooth and remove from the heat, then leave to cool slightly.

11. Beat the mascarpone until smooth. Fold the mascarpone and melted white chocolate into the cooled egg mixture until combined and smooth.

12. Using a long, serrated knife, slice the sponges in half horizontally. Place 1 sponge layer in the bottom of the 20cm springform tin, brush generously with the coffee syrup, then spread with 2 heaped tablespoons of the mascarpone mixture. Scatter with 1 tablespoon of the grated dark chocolate and top with another sponge layer.

13. Repeat the filling layers, and keep going (sponge, syrup, fillings, sponge, syrup, fillings) until you top with the final sponge. You will have mascarpone mixture and grated chocolate left over – cover each and chill until needed.

14. Press the stacked sponges together, cover and chill for at least 2 hours.

15. Remove the cake from the tin to a serving plate. Cover the top and sides with the remaining mascarpone mixture, then press the remaining grated chocolate onto the sides of the cake to cover.

16. To decorate, whip the cream to soft peaks. Spoon it into the piping bag fitted with a medium plain nozzle and pipe little blobs of cream all over the top of the cake. Scatter with the chocolate-coated coffee beans and lightly dust with cocoa powder to serve.

FOR THE CRYSTALLISED GOOSEBERRIES

18 small gooseberries, topped and tailed
1 egg white, very lightly beaten
caster sugar, for sprinkling

FOR THE ROASTED GOOSEBERRIES

400g ripe but firm gooseberries, topped and tailed
3 tbsp caster sugar, plus extra to taste if needed

FOR THE GINGER BISCUITS

75g self-raising flour
¾ tsp bicarbonate of soda
2 tsp ground ginger
30g caster sugar
40g unsalted butter, melted
30g golden syrup

FOR THE BISCUIT BASE

125g ginger biscuits (see above)
50g unsalted butter, melted

FOR THE CHEESECAKE FILLING

200g full-fat cream cheese
100g mascarpone
juice and finely grated zest of ½ unwaxed lemon
1 tbsp icing sugar
1 sheet platinum-grade gelatine, halved

TO DECORATE

6 sprigs of small gooseberry, lemon balm or mint leaves

YOU WILL NEED

4 baking trays, lined with baking paper
7cm-diameter dessert rings (4cm deep) x 6

Roasted Gooseberry Cheesecakes

Gooseberries are such a wonderfully seasonal treat. This simple but stunning dessert, with a homemade ginger-biscuit base, celebrates summer deliciously.

1. Make the crystallised gooseberries. Brush the gooseberries with the egg white and place on one of the lined baking trays. Sprinkle the sugar over the top to completely coat the fruit, then set aside in a warm place to dry.

2. Heat the oven to 180°C/160°C fan/Gas 4.

3. Make the roasted gooseberries. Place the gooseberries in a single layer in a roasting dish, sprinkle with the sugar and roast for 10 minutes, until just tender and still holding their shape. Remove from the oven and leave to cool.

4. Make the ginger biscuits. Increase the oven to 190°C/170°C fan/Gas 5. Sift the flour, bicarbonate of soda and ginger into a bowl, then stir in the sugar. Make a well in the centre and add the melted butter and the syrup. Stir until the mixture comes together to form a soft dough.

5. Divide the dough into 12 equal pieces and roll each into a ball. Transfer the balls, spacing them well apart, onto two of the lined baking trays, then flatten each slightly with the palm of your hand.

6. Bake the biscuits for 12–14 minutes, until golden and cracked on top. Leave to cool and firm up on the tray for 10 minutes, then transfer to a wire rack to cool completely.

7. Make the biscuit base. Place 125g of the cooled ginger biscuits into the bowl of a food processor and blitz to a fine crumb. Add the melted butter and pulse to combine. Place the 6 dessert rings on the remaining lined baking tray.

Continues overleaf

8. Divide the blitzed biscuit crumbs equally between the rings and press down with the end of a small rolling pin to compact into a biscuit base. Chill for 10 minutes.

9. Place half the roasted gooseberries in a sieve set over a measuring jug and press the juice through. You will need 100ml of the juice for the topping. Taste and add a little more sugar if you wish. Set aside in a small bowl.

10. Pick out the firmest gooseberries from the remaining roasted gooseberries and cut them in half. Arrange them, cut sides down, around the edge of the biscuit bases to form a ring, then spoon the remaining gooseberries into the centre of the ring.

11. For the cheesecake filling, gently stir the cream cheese, mascarpone, lemon zest and icing sugar together in a small bowl to combine. Set aside.

12. Place the lemon juice in a small, shallow bowl. Place both halves of the gelatine sheet in a shallow bowl with 3 tablespoons of water. Leave for 5 minutes to soften, then remove from the water and squeeze out any excess water.

13. Place one soaked gelatine sheet half into the lemon juice and the other half into the gooseberry juice.

14. Warm the lemon juice in the microwave for 15 seconds until the gelatine has dissolved (or place the bowl over a pan of simmering water). Remove from the heat and leave to cool slightly, then stir into the cream-cheese mixture. Spoon this mixture over the gooseberries in the dessert rings leaving about 3mm height at the top for a thin jelly layer. Level with the back of a spoon until smooth.

15. Warm the gooseberry juice in the microwave for 15 seconds, until the gelatine has dissolved (or place the bowl over a pan of simmering water). Remove from the heat, leave to cool slightly, then pour a thin layer on top of each dessert. Chill for at least 2 hours to set.

16. To serve, remove the rings from the cheesecakes and decorate with the crystallised gooseberries and leaves.

FOR THE CHOUX
125ml whole milk
100g unsalted butter, cubed
1 rounded tsp caster sugar
good pinch of salt
165g plain flour, sifted
5 eggs, beaten

FOR THE NOUGATINE
150g flaked almonds
225g caster sugar
15g unsalted butter

FOR THE CUSTARD FILLING
500ml whole milk
150g caster sugar
6 egg yolks
3 tbsp cornflour
1 tsp vanilla paste
pinch of salt
150ml double cream
2 tbsp homemade or
    good-quality lemon curd

FOR THE RASPBERRY JELLY
150g frozen raspberries
1 tbsp caster sugar
1 sheet platinum-grade
    leaf gelatine

FOR THE CARAMEL
500g caster sugar

TO DECORATE
200g raspberries
2 tbsp raspberry pearl sugar

YOU WILL NEED
large piping bag fitted
    with a large plain nozzle
2 baking sheets,
    greased, then lined
    with baking paper
23cm springform cake tin,
    greased, then base-lined
    with baking paper
medium piping bag fitted
    with a small plain nozzle
small piping bag fitted
    with a small plain
    or writing nozzle

Serves
12

Hands on
2 hours

Bake
30 mins

Croquembouche

This tower of caramel-coated choux buns is often served at French weddings, but is a stunning dinner party dessert. The name translates to 'crunch in the mouth', which refers to the crisp coating on each bun. You can prepare the buns and the nougatine base up to two days in advance. Store the buns in an airtight box, but crisp them up and cool again before filling; simply wrap the nougatine in baking paper. Similarly, you can prepare and chill the custard and raspberry fillings up to 24 hours ahead. Serve soon after assembling, before the caramel starts to soften.

1. Heat the oven to 200°C/180°C fan/Gas 6.

2. Make the choux buns. Pour the milk, butter, sugar and salt into a saucepan with 125ml water. Place over a medium heat and stir to melt the butter, then bring the mixture to a rolling boil. Immediately slide the pan off the heat, quickly add the flour and beat vigorously until the batter is smooth.

3. Return the pan to a medium heat, beating continuously for 30 seconds, until the mixture is glossy and cleanly leaves the sides of the pan.

4. Tip the mixture into a bowl and leave to cool for 5–10 minutes. Gradually, add the eggs, beating well until the batter is silky smooth and reluctantly drops off the spoon.

5. Scoop the dough into the large piping bag fitted with the large plain nozzle and pipe 35–40 buns, each about the size of a small walnut, on each lined baking sheet (70–80 buns altogether). Leave a little space between each bun to allow for spreading during baking.

6. Bake the choux buns for 25–30 minutes, until puffed up, crisp and golden brown. Using a wooden skewer, make a hole in the underside of each bun to allow the steam to escape and leave the buns on the baking sheets to cool completely. (Leave the oven on.)

Continues overleaf

7. While the buns are cooling, make the nougatine base. Toast the flaked almonds on a baking tray on the lowest shelf in the oven for 3–4 minutes, until light golden.

8. Tip the sugar into a heavy-based saucepan, add 2 tablespoons of water and place over a low heat to dissolve the sugar, gently swirling the pan from time to time (but don't stir), until syrupy.

9. Increase the heat, bring the syrup to the boil and continue to cook, without stirring, until it turns an amber colour. Add the flaked almonds and butter and stir to thoroughly combine.

10. Working quickly, scoop the nougatine into the springform tin and, using a lightly oiled spoon, spread into an even layer. Leave to cool and harden.

11. Make the custard filling. Heat the milk in a heavy-based saucepan over a medium heat to just below boiling point. Meanwhile, whisk together the sugar, egg yolks, cornflour, vanilla and salt in a heatproof mixing bowl until thoroughly combined and slightly paler in colour.

12. Pour the hot milk into the bowl containing the egg-yolk mixture, whisking continuously until smooth. Return the mixture to the pan and cook over a low heat, whisking, for about 2 minutes, until it comes to the boil and thickens. If you can still taste the cornflour, continue cooking for a further 10–20 seconds.

13. Pour the custard through a sieve into a clean bowl, then cover the surface with baking paper to prevent a skin forming. Leave to cool completely, then chill until ready to use.

14. Make the raspberry jelly. Tip the frozen raspberries into a small saucepan, add the sugar and 1 tablespoon of water and cook over a low–medium heat for about 5 minutes, until the raspberries have softened and the resulting juice has reduced slightly.

15. Meanwhile, soak the gelatine leaf in cold water for 5 minutes, until soft. Push the warm raspberry mixture through a nylon sieve into a bowl. Drain the gelatine leaf, squeeze out any excess water and add to the raspberry purée, then stir until dissolved. Leave to cool, then cover, and chill until set.

16. Continue making the custard filling. Whisk the cream to stiff peaks and fold it into the chilled custard, along with the lemon curd. Spoon into the medium piping bag fitted with a small plain nozzle. Pipe the custard into the choux buns, using the hole you made on the undersides for steam to escape and taking care not to overfill.

17. Spoon the raspberry jelly into the small piping bag with the small plain or writing nozzle. Pipe the jelly into the middle of the custard filling in each choux bun. Chill the filled buns for 30 minutes.

18. Meanwhile, make the caramel. Heat 400g of the sugar with 4 tablespoons of water in a heavy-based saucepan over a low heat, gently swirling the pan from time to time (but don't stir), until the sugar dissolves.

19. Increase the heat, bring the syrup to the boil and continue to cook, without stirring, until it turns an amber colour, then quickly slide the pan off the heat.

20. Working quickly and using tongs, dip the top of each choux bun into the caramel and return to the lined baking sheet. Warm the caramel over a low heat if it starts to harden.

21. To assemble the croquembouche, remove the nougatine base from the tin and place on a serving plate. Arrange the choux buns in a neat, tight circle on top, sticking them to the base with a little of the caramel and leaving a 2cm border around the edge.

22. Dipping each bun into the caramel to act as a glue as you go, arrange the choux buns on top of the first layer, then continue stacking the buns, creating a tall cone shape. Arrange fresh raspberries and pearl sugar in between the choux buns.

23. Make a second caramel using the remaining 100g caster sugar and 1 tablespoon of water using the instructions in steps 18 and 19.

24. Plunge the base of the pan into cold water to stop the cooking process, then, while the caramel is still liquid, using the tines of a fork, pull the caramel from the pan into thin, wispy strands and swirl them around the croquembouche to encase the choux tower. Warm the caramel over a low heat to soften again when you need to.

FOR THE APPLE PURÉE
1 eating apple, peeled,
    cored and sliced

FOR THE SPONGE
350g plain flour, sifted
90g cocoa powder, sifted
2¼ tsp bicarbonate of soda
450g light brown soft sugar
135ml light olive oil
1½ tsp vanilla paste
570ml almond milk
2¼ tsp apple cider vinegar
3 ripe but firm pears
    (such as Comice, Williams
    or Conference), peeled,
    cored and sliced

FOR THE GANACHE
150g vegan dark chocolate
75ml almond milk

FOR THE VANILLA FROSTING
125g icing sugar, sifted
75g vegan spread
1 tsp vanilla paste
1 tbsp almond milk
    (optional)

TO DECORATE
20 edible flowers
    (such as pansies,
    violas and calendulas)
micro lemon balm leaves
thyme sprigs
pistachio kernels,
    finely chopped
handful of fresh berries
    and cherries

YOU WILL NEED
20cm sandwich tins x 2,
    oiled, then base-lined
    with baking paper
medium piping bag
    fitted with a large
    plain nozzle (optional)

*Serves
8–10*

*Hands on
45 mins*

*Bake
40 mins*

Sticky Chocolate and Pear Fudge Cake

The addition of pear to this super-sticky, chocolate layer cake lifts it from fudgy cake to decadent dessert. Try adding a caramel sauce between the layers and sprinkling with candied nuts for an even more indulgent cake, if you wish.

1. Make the apple purée. Place the apple in a pan with 2 teaspoons of water. Cook over a low heat, gently simmering for about 5–10 minutes, until soft. Remove from the heat, leave to cool slightly, then blitz with a hand-held stick blender to a purée. Set aside.

2. Make the sponge. Mix the flour, cocoa powder and bicarbonate of soda in a large bowl. Heat the oven to 180°C/160°C fan/Gas 4.

3. Whisk the sugar, olive oil, vanilla, almond milk and vinegar in a stand mixer fitted with the whisk, on medium speed for 1 minute, until combined. Stir in 2 tablespoons of the apple purée and whisk for another 1 minute. Add the flour mixture and whisk on low speed until combined and smooth. Half-fill each of the sandwich tins with the mixture and arrange the pear slices on top. Pour the remaining mixture over the pears to cover. Bake for 35–40 minutes, until risen and firm to the touch. Leave in the tins to cool completely.

4. Meanwhile, make the ganache. Melt the chocolate and almond milk in a heatproof bowl set over a pan of barely simmering water. Stir until smooth and shiny, and remove from the heat.

5. Make the vanilla frosting. Beat the icing sugar, vegan spread and vanilla in a stand mixer fitted with the beater, on medium speed for 2–3 minutes, until light and creamy. Add a little almond milk to loosen if necessary. Spoon into the piping bag, if using.

6. Turn out the cakes. Pipe the frosting on top of one sponge (or spread with a palette knife). Top with the second sponge, then pour over the ganache and make lines back and forth in it with a dessertspoon. Decorate with flowers, leaves, pistachios and berries.

FOR THE PAVLOVA
6 large egg whites
350g caster sugar
good pinch of salt
1 tbsp gluten-free cornflour
1 tsp cider or white
    wine vinegar
1 tsp vanilla paste

FOR THE FILLING
400ml double cream
200ml crème fraîche
50g icing sugar, sifted,
    plus extra for dusting
1 tsp vanilla paste
seeds of 4 cardamom
    pods, finely ground
1 tsp finely grated
    unwaxed orange zest
8–10 figs, cut into
    thin wedges
300g raspberries
seeds of 1 pomegranate

TO SERVE
25g flaked almonds, toasted
25g unsalted, shelled
    pistachios, nibbed or
    roughly chopped

YOU WILL NEED
large piping bag fitted
    with a large star nozzle
3 baking sheets, lined
    with baking paper,
    each sheet drawn
    with a 20cm circle

Gluten Free

Serves
8-10

Hands on
30 mins

Bake
50 mins

plus chilling

Fig, Pomegranate and Cardamom Pavlova

The fig, pomegranate and cardamom, along with the topping of pistachios and almonds, give this version of a pavlova a Middle Eastern twist. If you want to make two tiers, rather than three, make thicker meringue discs and increase the baking time by 10 minutes.

1. Heat the oven to 180°C/160°C fan/Gas 4.

2. Whisk the egg whites, sugar and salt in a stand mixer fitted with a whisk, on high speed for 8–10 minutes, until the mixture is very thick, glossy and completely smooth between your fingertips.

3. Sift the cornflour onto the meringue, add the vinegar and vanilla and mix for 20 seconds to combine. Spoon into the piping bag.

4. Turn the baking paper on the baking sheets so that the drawn circles are on the undersides. Pipe 1 meringue disc on each sheet of baking paper, using the drawn circles as a guide.

5. Bake for 3 minutes, then reduce the heat to 120°C/100°C fan/Gas ¾ and bake for 45 minutes, until the meringue is crisp on the outside and marshmallowy in the middle. Turn off the oven and leave the meringues to cool for 1 hour, then leave the door ajar until cold.

6. Make the filling. Whip together the cream, crème fraîche, icing sugar, vanilla, cardamom and orange zest to soft peaks.

7. Carefully slide one of the meringues off the baking paper onto a serving plate. Spoon one third of the whipped-cream mixture on top. Scatter a third of the figs over the cream and top with one third of the raspberries and pomegranate seeds.

8. Repeat this layering of meringue, cream and fruit twice more, arranging the fruit decoratively on the top layer. Scatter with the almonds and pistachios and dust with icing sugar, to serve.

FOR THE SYRUP
200g caster sugar
large pinch of ground
    cardamom
small pinch of saffron
¼ tsp rose water

FOR THE PURIS
60g clarified butter
egg-yellow food-colouring
    gel (optional)
250g plain flour,
    plus extra if needed
1 tbsp whole milk,
    plus extra if needed
100g full-fat natural yogurt
vegetable oil, for frying

YOU WILL NEED
5cm round cutter

*Makes
about 50*

*Hands on
1 hour*

plus resting

*Fry
15 mins*

BAKER'S FAVOURITE

Makbul's Dahi Puris

The sublime rose flavour of the syrup coupled with the tang of yogurt in these dahi puris makes for a delicious sweet bite at the end of a meal (or even a snack to have with a cup of tea at other times of day). During my childhood, my mum would whip these up to keep us quiet for a while!

1. Make the syrup. Heat the sugar, cardamom and saffron with 180ml water over a medium heat, stirring, until the sugar dissolves. Reduce the heat and simmer for 5 minutes, until it becomes syrupy. Remove from the heat and stir in the rose water. Leave to cool completely.

2. Meanwhile, make the puris. Melt the clarified butter in a small pan over a low heat (or use a microwave) and stir in a little yellow food colouring, if using. Sift the flour into a mixing bowl, then add the melted butter and mix with your fingers until combined.

3. Gently warm the milk and yogurt in a small saucepan. Stir into the flour, then bring the mixture together with your hands, kneading to form a smooth but not sticky dough (don't over-knead), adding more flour or milk if needed. Cover the dough and rest for 1 hour.

4. To shape the puris, divide the dough into 4 equal pieces. One piece at a time, roll out the dough until about 2mm thick. Using the 5cm cutter, cut out as many puris as you can, transferring them to a baking sheet as you go (it doesn't matter if they overlap).

5. Pour oil into a wok or a deep pan to about 3cm deep and place over a medium heat. Heat until a small piece of dough bubbles as soon as it is dropped into the oil and rises to the surface after a few seconds. In batches to just cover the surface of the oil, fry the puris, turning, for 30–45 seconds, until puffed up and golden. If they brown too quickly, reduce the heat. Set each batch aside to drain on kitchen paper.

6. Dip the fried puris in the cooled syrup until generously covered on both sides, then place on a plate to drain before serving. (The puris will store at room temperature for up to 2 days.)

125g 70% dark chocolate,
   roughly chopped
125g 54% dark chocolate,
   roughly chopped
150g unsalted butter, cubed
6 eggs, separated
150g caster sugar
100g light brown soft sugar
1 tsp vanilla paste or extract
pinch of salt
1 tbsp ground almonds
1 tbsp gluten-free cornflour
icing sugar, for dusting
a few raspberries, to serve
   (optional)

YOU WILL NEED
23cm springform tin,
   greased, then base-lined
   with baking paper

Serves
8-10

Hands on
30 mins

Bake
30 mins

Chocolate Torte

*This rich chocolate torte uses two types of dark chocolate,
each with a different percentage of cocoa solids, to give the
perfect balance of bitter and sweet. If you prefer a more intense
chocolate flavour, feel free to use only 70%-cocoa solids chocolate.
Dust the torte with icing sugar to decorate, and serve with a bowl
of softly whipped cream and fresh berries alongside.*

1. Heat the oven to 170°C/150°C fan/Gas 3.

2. Melt both types of chocolate and the butter in a large, heatproof
bowl set over a pan of barely simmering water. Stir until smooth,
remove from the heat, then leave to cool for 2–3 minutes.

3. Whisk the egg yolks, both types of sugar and the vanilla in a stand
mixer fitted with a whisk until thick and mousse-like, and the mixture
leaves a ribbon trail when you lift the whisk.

4. Using a balloon whisk or an electric hand whisk, whisk the egg
whites and salt in a large, clean bowl to stiff peaks.

5. Using a large metal spoon, fold the melted chocolate mixture
into the egg-yolk mixture until combined. Add the ground almonds
and cornflour and mix again until smooth.

6. Spoon one third of the egg whites into the chocolate mixture
and lightly fold in, trying not to knock out too much air, then fold
in another third. Add the remaining egg whites and fold in until
there are no streaks of egg white remaining.

7. Carefully spoon or pour the mixture into the lined tin. Bake
on the middle shelf for 30 minutes, until risen and the top is set,
cooked and cracked slightly, but with a slight wobble underneath.
Leave to cool in the tin to room temperature.

8. Remove the torte from the tin and dust with icing sugar.
Serve with raspberries alongside, if you wish.

FOR THE SPONGE
500g unsalted butter, softened
500g caster sugar
2 tsp vanilla paste
¼ tsp salt
10 large eggs
150g plain flour, sifted
200ml soured cream
520g self-raising flour, sifted
90ml whole milk
200g white chocolate, finely chopped
300g raspberries

FOR THE GANACHE
200g white chocolate
200ml double cream

FOR THE RASPBERRY COMPOTE
150g raspberries
100g caster sugar

FOR THE SYRUP
100g caster sugar
1 tsp vanilla paste

FOR THE BUTTERCREAM
450g unsalted butter, at room temperature
840g icing sugar, sifted
6 tbsp whole milk
2 tsp vanilla paste

TO DECORATE
edible flowers (such as pansies, violas, roses and bellis)
fresh raspberries
micro-mint tips or lemon balm sprigs
freeze-dried raspberry pieces

YOU WILL NEED
25cm springform tins or deep sandwich tins x 3, greased, then lined (base and sides) with baking paper
3 medium piping bags, each fitted with a large plain nozzle
25cm cake board
cake scraper

Serves 16–20

Hands on 1½ hours

Bake 40 mins

Raspberry and White Chocolate Ombre Cake

These vanilla and soured-cream sponges are dotted with plump raspberries and white chocolate chips, then layered with a fresh raspberry buttercream, raspberry compote and white chocolate ganache. It's a cake – bit it's so much a dessert, too.

1. Heat the oven to 160°C/140°C fan/Gas 3.

2. Make the sponge. Beat the butter, sugar, vanilla and salt in a stand mixer fitted with the beater, on a medium speed for 10 minutes, until pale and fluffy, scraping down the sides of the bowl from time to time.

3. Add the eggs, one at a time, beating well between each addition, and adding a spoonful of the plain flour if the mixture starts to curdle. Stir in the soured cream.

4. Mix the remaining plain flour with the self-raising and fold this gently into the cake mixture. Add the milk and the white chocolate.

5. Divide the mixture equally between the lined tins. Scatter the raspberries over the surface of each sponge and lightly press the raspberries into the mixture.

6. Bake for 35–40 minutes, until the sponges are golden and risen, and a skewer inserted into the centres comes out clean.

7. Meanwhile, make the ganache. Melt the chocolate and cream in a heatproof bowl set over a pan of barely simmering water. Stir until smooth, then remove from the heat. Leave to cool completely (the ganache should be softly set, not firm).

8. Make the raspberry compote. Tip the raspberries, sugar and 1 tablespoon of water into a small saucepan. Bring slowly to the boil, stirring until the sugar dissolves, then reduce the heat and simmer for 10 minutes, or until the raspberries break down to a purée.

Continues overleaf

9. Crush the raspberries with the back of a spoon to release their colour. If you prefer a seedless compote, pass the mixture through a sieve into a bowl (discard the contents of the sieve). Reserve 3 tablespoons of the compote to colour the buttercream. Leave to cool.

10. Make the syrup. Pour 100ml water into a pan with the sugar and vanilla and place over a low heat to dissolve the sugar, gently swirling the pan from time to time (but don't stir), until syrupy. Remove from the heat and leave to cool.

11. When the sponges are ready, prick holes in the top of each with a cocktail stick and generously brush the syrup over. Leave in the tins to cool completely.

12. Make the buttercream. Beat the butter in a stand mixer fitted with the beater, on medium–high speed for 5 minutes, until pale and fluffy. Add the icing sugar in 6 batches each with 1 tablespoon of the milk, beating well after each addition. Add the vanilla paste and beat to a spreadable, pale buttercream.

13. Divide the buttercream into 3 bowls. Add teaspoons of the reserved raspberry compote, in different quantities, to two of the bowls to make different shades of pink. Leave the remaining buttercream plain. Spoon each into a piping bag fitted with a large plain nozzle.

14. Pipe dots of buttercream onto the 25cm cake board and place one sponge on the board. Spread a layer of the plain buttercream over the top, evenly to the edges, then pipe a ring around the edge.

15. Whisk the white chocolate ganache with an electric hand whisk until fluffy. Spread half in the middle of the sponge, within the piped buttercream ring, and top with half the raspberry compote. Place the second sponge on top and repeat with the buttercream and raspberry compote, then top with the third sponge.

16. Pipe a generous layer of plain buttercream over the top layer and make a swirl pattern with a large offset spatula.

17. Pipe thick stripes of the buttercream in all three shades, starting with dark pink at the bottom and moving to plain at the top, around the side of the cake. Scrape away the excess with a cake scraper to achieve a semi-naked finish. Decorate with fresh edible flowers, preferably roses, bellis, violas and pansies, a few fresh raspberries, and the micro-mint or lemon balm. Sprinkle with freeze-dried raspberry pieces to finish.

Conversion Tables

WEIGHT

METRIC	IMPERIAL	METRIC	IMPERIAL	METRIC	IMPERIAL	METRIC	IMPERIAL
25g	1oz	200g	7oz	425g	15oz	800g	1lb 12oz
50g	2oz	225g	8oz	450g	1lb	850g	1lb 14oz
75g	2½oz	250g	9oz	500g	1lb 2oz	900g	2lb
85g	3oz	280g	10oz	550g	1lb 4oz	950g	2lb 2oz
100g	4oz	300g	11oz	600g	1lb 5oz	1kg	2lb 4oz
125g	4½oz	350g	12oz	650g	1lb 7oz		
140g	5oz	375g	13oz	700g	1lb 9oz		
175g	6oz	400g	14oz	750g	1lb 10oz		

VOLUME

METRIC	IMPERIAL	METRIC	IMPERIAL	METRIC	IMPERIAL	METRIC	IMPERIAL
30ml	1fl oz	150ml	¼ pint	300ml	½ pint	500ml	18fl oz
50ml	2fl oz	175ml	6fl oz	350ml	12fl oz	600ml	1 pint
75ml	2½fl oz	200ml	7fl oz	400ml	14fl oz	700ml	1¼ pints
100ml	3½fl oz	225ml	8fl oz	425ml	¾ pint	850ml	1½ pints
125ml	4fl oz	250ml	9fl oz	450ml	16fl oz	1 litre	1¾ pints

US CUP

INGREDIENTS	1 CUP	¾ CUP	⅔ CUP	½ CUP	⅓ CUP	¼ CUP	2 TBSP
Brown sugar	180g	135g	120g	90g	60g	45g	23g
Butter	240g	180g	160g	120g	80g	60g	30g
Cornflour (corn starch)	120g	90g	80g	60g	40g	30g	15g
Flour	120g	90g	80g	60g	40g	30g	15g
Icing sugar (powdered/confectioner's)	100g	75g	70g	50g	35g	25g	13g
Nuts (chopped)	150g	110g	100g	75g	50g	40g	20g
Nuts (ground)	120g	90g	80g	60g	40g	30g	15g
Oats	90g	65g	60g	45g	30g	22g	11g
Raspberries	120g	90g	80g	60g	40g	30g	--
Salt	300g	230g	200g	150g	100g	75g	40g
Sugar (granulated)	200g	150g	130g	100g	65g	50g	25g
Sugar (caster/superfine)	225g	170g	150g	115g	75g	55g	30g
Sultanas/raisins	200g	150g	130g	100g	65g	50g	22g
Water/milk	250ml	180ml	150ml	120ml	75ml	60ml	30ml

LINEAR

METRIC	IMPERIAL	METRIC	IMPERIAL	METRIC	IMPERIAL	METRIC	IMPERIAL
2.5cm	1 in	7.5cm	3 in	13cm	5 in	20cm	8 in
3cm	1¼ in	8cm	3¼ in	14cm	5½ in	21cm	8¼ in
4cm	1½ in	9cm	3½ in	15cm	6 in	22cm	8½ in
5cm	2 in	9.5cm	3¾ in	16cm	6¼ in	23cm	9 in
5.5cm	2¼ in	10cm	4 in	17cm	6½ in	24cm	9½ in
6cm	2½ in	11cm	4¼ in	18cm	7 in	25cm	10 in
7cm	2¾ in	12cm	4½ in	19cm	7½ in		

SPOON MEASURES

METRIC	IMPERIAL
5ml	1 tsp
10ml	2 tsp
15ml	1 tbsp
30ml	2 tbsp
45ml	3 tbsp
60ml	4 tbsp
75ml	5 tbsp

COOK'S NOTES

Oven temperatures: Ovens vary – not only from brand to brand, but from the front to the back of the oven, as well as (in a non-fan oven) between the top and bottom shelves. Invest in a cooking thermometer if you can. Always preheat, and use dry oven gloves.

Eggs: Eggs are medium and should be at room temperature, unless specified. Some recipes may contain raw or partially cooked eggs. Pregnant women, the elderly, babies and toddlers, and people who are unwell should be aware of these recipes.

Butter: In the recipes, 'softened butter' means to soften to room temperature, unless otherwise specified. You should be able to leave an indentation with your fingertip when you press down.

Herbs and fruit: Use fresh herbs and fresh, medium-sized fruit unless the recipe specifies otherwise.

Salt: If a recipe calls for a small, or hard-to-weigh amount, a ½ teaspoon fine salt weighs 2.5g, and a ¼ teaspoon weighs 1.25g. If you're using sea salt it is best to crush the flakes into a fine powder before measuring and adding to your recipe (unless specified).

Spoon measures: All teaspoons and tablespoons are level unless otherwise stated.

Allergies or special diets: We want you to share these recipes with your loved ones and your community as often as possible. Please be aware, though, that some recipes contain allergens. If you are baking for others, do check before you share.

Baking Tips and Techniques

Use these tips and techniques to help you get the best results from your bakes.

FOLDING IN

This is a way to combine two (or more) ingredients as delicately as possible so you don't knock out all the air. A large metal spoon or a rubber spatula is best for folding.

Cut down through the mixture to the bottom of the bowl, turn the spoon or spatula upwards and draw it up, then flip it over so the mixture flops onto the surface. Give the bowl a quarter turn and repeat to combine.

RUBBING IN

This is a way to combine butter and flour and add air when making pastry and simple cake mixtures. Use only your fingertips and thumbs (which are cooler than your palms) – try to keep your palms clean.

Pick up a little of the butter and flour mixture, lift your hands and gently rub your fingers and thumbs together to combine the mixture as it falls. Keep doing this until the mixture has a crumb-like consistency.

MELTING CHOCOLATE

Chop or break up the chocolate into equal pieces. Put it into a heatproof bowl and set this over a pan of steaming hot, simmering, but not boiling water – don't let the base of the bowl touch the water. As the chocolate softens, stir it gently. It is ready to use as soon as it is liquid and smooth, around 30°C (if you have a cooking thermometer). You can also melt chocolate in the microwave. For best results, microwave in 10-second bursts, checking and stirring each time.

RIBBON STAGE

Whisking eggs and sugar thoroughly builds up a thick mass of tiny air bubbles that forms the structure of a cake. Use a large bowl – after 4–5 minutes of whisking on high speed, the initial volume of eggs and sugar will increase five-fold. The ribbon stage occurs when you lift the whisk out of the bowl and the mixture on it falls back onto the surface to make a distinct, thick, ribbon-like trail.

BLIND BAKING

This means to bake an unfilled tart so the pastry is cooked before adding the filling. Line the pastry case with the baking paper (cut to size and crumpled up to make it more flexible) and fill with ceramic baking beans, rice or dried beans. Bake as stated in the recipe (or about 12–15 minutes, until set and firm). Remove the paper and beans, then return the pastry case to the oven and bake for a further 5–10 minutes, until the pastry is thoroughly cooked and starting to colour.

KNEADING BREAD DOUGH

Kneading – or working – a dough develops the gluten in the flour to create a neat structure that stretches around the bubbles of carbon dioxide gas, released as the yeast or other raising agent activates in the heat of the oven. The dough will rise slowly, and set.

To knead by hand, lightly dust the worktop and your fingers with flour, or grease with a teaspoon of oil. Turn out the dough onto the worktop. Hold down one end with your hand and use the other hand to pull and stretch out the dough away from you. Gather the dough back into a ball again and give it a quarter turn, then repeat the stretching and gathering back. As you knead you'll notice the dough starts to feel pliable, and then stretchy, then very elastic and silky smooth. Nearly all doughs need 10 minutes of thorough kneading to give you the best results. (Under-kneading can produce a soggy, flat or dense loaf.)

To knead in a stand mixer, use a dough hook on the lowest possible speed and knead for about 5 minutes. While it's almost impossible to over-knead by hand (your arms will give out first), you can stretch the gluten beyond repair in a mixer, which means the dough won't rise well at all.

To test if the dough has been kneaded enough, take a small piece and stretch it between your fingers to make a thin, translucent sheet. If it won't stretch out or it tears easily, knead a while longer.

RISING AND PROVING
Most recipes require the dough to rise until doubled in size. For the best results, place the dough in a moist, warm spot. A room temperature of 20–24°C is ideal – if the room is too hot, the yeast will grow too rapidly and the dough will become distorted (and maybe develop a slight aftertaste); too cool and the yeast develops more slowly (although this can give a richer flavour and chewier crumb and crust). Proving is the last period of rising prior to baking, after shaping

a bread dough. The time this takes (usually to double in size again) depends on the temperature of the dough (some, like brioche, are chilled before shaping), and how lively your yeast is. To test whether or not the dough is properly proved, gently prod it: if it springs back, it's not quite ready; if it returns to its original state fairly slowly, or if there's a very slight dent, it's ready.

KNOCKING BACK BREAD DOUGH
Knocking back or punching down risen dough usually happens after rising and before shaping and proving. It breaks up the large gas bubbles that have formed within it to make smaller, finer bubbles that expand more evenly during baking, causing a more even rise. Use your knuckles to punch down the dough. Some bakers fold or flop the dough over on itself a few times.

PERFECTING A BREAD CRUST
First, make sure the oven is thoroughly heated, so the dough quickly puffs (called 'oven-spring') and then sets evenly.

For a crisp upper crust, create a burst of steam to keep the surface of the bread moist, helping the bread to rise easily. Once the surface has set, the moisture evaporates, leaving a crisp finish. To create the steam, put an empty roasting tin on the floor of the oven as you heat the oven up. Then, immediately as you put in the unbaked loaf, pour cold water or throw a handful of ice cubes into the hot tin. Close the door to trap in the steam.

For a crisp base, put a baking sheet or baking stone in the oven to heat up. Then carefully transfer your loaf (in a tin or on a sheet of baking paper) onto the hot baking sheet or stone for baking.

Inspire me . . .

Use this visual index when you need inspiration for a bake by type or special diet, or when you specifically want a judge's recipe to impress. Note that, because sweet bakes tend anyway to be vegetarian, we've separated out savoury vegetarian recipes only into a category of their own.

BISCUITS

Chai Crackle Cookies (p.32)

Mini Orange and Ginger Florentines (p.49)

Chocolate Panforte (p.55)

Good-dog Biscuits (p.63)

Cookie Bunting (p.83)

Prue's Coconut Macaroons (p.88)

Thumbprint Biscuits (p.99)

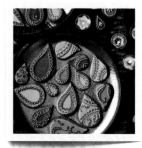

Iced and Spiced Biscuits (p.117)

Spritz Cookies (p.137)

Ricciarelli (p.194)

Kitchen Sink Cookies (p.197)

Peanut and Caramel Millionaire's Shortbread (p.208)

BREADS

Paul's Chocolate Babka (p.35)

Devonshire Splits (p.40)

Onion and Rosemary
Potato Focaccia (p.52)

Hermine's Ham, Cheese and
Chive Couronnes (p.56)

Steamed Bun Pandas (p.73)

Paul's Rainbow-coloured
Bagels (p.81)

Malt Loaf (p.102)

Pesto Star Bread (p.121)

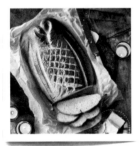

Duivekater (p.132)

Sticky Pear and Cinnamon
Buns (p.165)

Ring Doughnuts (p.182)

Paul's Jam and Custard
Doughnuts (p.201)

Sura's Parsley, Feta and Spinach
Turkish Pastries (p.210)

Sourdough (p.219)

Herby Garlic Rolls (p.241)

CAKES

Mini Lemon and Pistachio Battenbergs (p.37)

Marc's Chocolate Brownie Drip Cake (p.43)

Butterfly Cakes (p.92)

Fruit and Flowers Wedding Cake (p.113)

Laura's Chocolate and Salted Caramel Cake (p.123)

Novelty Frog Cake (p.127)

Rhubarb, Rose and Pistachio Layer Cake (p.129)

Strawberry and Elderflower Cake (p.135)

Prue's Mille Crêpe Cake (p.141)

Hummingbird Cake (p.143)

Christmas Log Cake (p.147)

Lottie's Black Forest Gâteau (p.163)

Paul's Pineapple Upside-down Cakes (p.175)

Our Chocolate Cake (p.181)

Lemon, Lime and Ginger Drizzle Cakes (p.207)

Sticky Toffee Apple Cakes (p.217)

CAKES *CONTINUED*

Tiramisù Cake (p.249)

Sticky Chocolate and Pear Fudge Cake (p.258)

Raspberry and White Chocolate Ombre Cake (p.267)

DAIRY-FREE

Ricciarelli (p.194)

Sourdough (p.219)

GLUTEN-FREE

Roasted Butternut Squash and Goat's Cheese Tart (p.45)

Granola Bars (p.58)

Button Meringues (p.79)

Prue's Coconut Macaroons (p.88)

Cheese Gougères (p.97)

Rhubarb, Rose and Pistachio Layer Cake (p.129)

Strawberry and Elderflower Cake (p.135)

Ricciarelli (p.194)

Peter's Red Berry Delice (p.243)

Fig, Pomegranate and Cardamom Pavlova (p.261)

Chocolate Torte (p.264)

JUDGES' RECIPES

Paul's Chocolate Babka (p.35)

Paul's Rainbow-coloured Bagels (p.81)

Prue's Coconut Macaroons (p.88)

Prue's Mille Crêpe Cake (p.141)

Paul's Pineapple Upside-down Cakes (p.175)

Prue's Sussex Pond Puddings (p.185)

Paul's Jam and Custard Doughnuts (p.201)

Prue's Raspberry and Salted Caramel Éclairs (p.213)

PUDS & DESSERTS

Sticky Toffee Puddings (p.50)

Button Meringues (p.79)

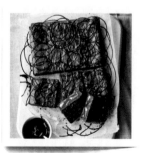

Dave's Triple-chocolate Brownies (p.94)

Cherry and Chocolate Baked Alaska (p.109)

Prue's Mille Crèpe Cake (p.141)

Pastis Gascon (p.154)

Lemon, Lime and Passion Fruit Meringue Pie (p.157)

Lottie's Black Forest Gâteau (p.163)

Paris-Brest (p.169)

Pandowdy Swamp Pie (p.171)

Paul's Pineapple Upside-down Cakes (p.175)

Prue's Sussex Pond Puddings (p.185)

Paul's Jam and Custard Doughnuts (p.201)

Peter's Red Berry Delice (p.243)

Basque Cheesecake (p.246)

Tiramisù Cake (p.249)

Roasted Gooseberry Cheesecakes (p.251)

Croquembouche (p.255)

Sticky Chocolate and Pear Fudge Cake (p.258)

Fig, Pomegranate and Cardamom Pavlova (p.261)

Makbul's Dahi Puris (p.262)

Chocolate Torte (p.264)

Raspberry and White Chocolate Ombre Cake (p.267)

SAVOURY

Roasted Butternut Squash and Goat's Cheese Tart (p.45)

Onion and Rosemary Potato Focaccia (p.52)

Hermine's Ham, Cheese and Chive Couronnes (p.56)

Loriea's Jamaican Beef Patties (p.61)

Steamed Bun Pandas (p.73)

Cheese Twists (p.75)

Paul's Rainbow-coloured Bagels (p.81)

Mini Pizzas (p.87)

Cheese Gougères (p.97)

Pesto Star Bread (p.121)

Chicken and Leek Pie (p.159)

Linda's Flaky Black Pudding Sausage Rolls (p.177)

SAVOURY CONTINUED

Mark's Chicken Tagine Pies (p.187)

Sura's Parsley, Feta and Spinach Turkish Pastries (p.210)

Sourdough (p.219)

Cheese and Spring Onion Scones (p.227)

Rowan's Salmon and Horseradish Vol au Vents (p.233)

Spinach, Fennel and Feta Galette (p.235)

Hot 'n' Spicy Quiches (p.239)

Herby Garlic Rolls (p.241)

SWEET PASTRY & PÂTISSÉRIE

Pastis Gascon (p.154)

Sticky Pear and Cinnamon Buns (p.165)

Paris-Brest (p.169)

Pandowdy Swamp Pie (p.171)

Apricot and Almond Tarts (p.203)

Prue's Raspberry and Salted Caramel Éclairs (p.213)

Croquembouche (p.255)

Makbul's Dahi Puris (p.262)

Inspire me . . .   **281**

TRAYBAKES

Granola Bars (p.58)

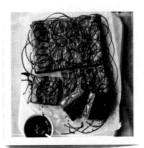

Rocky Road (p.70)

Dave's Triple-chocolate
Brownies (p.94)

Peanut Butter and
Raspberry Blondies (p.198)

Peanut and Caramel
Millionaire's Shortbread (p.208)

Speculoos Cheesecake
Squares (p.224)

VEGAN

Onion and Rosemary
Potato Focaccia (p.52)

Granola Bars (p.58)

Steamed Bun Pandas (p.73)

Hummingbird Cake (p.143)

Sticky Toffee Apple Cakes
(p.217)

Sticky Chocolate and Pear
Fudge Cake (p.258)

VEGETARIAN SAVOURY

Roasted Butternut Squash and Goat's Cheese Tart (p.45)

Onion and Rosemary Potato Focaccia (p.52)

Steamed Bun Pandas (p.73)

Cheese Twists (p.75)

Paul's Rainbow-coloured Bagels (p.81)

Mini Pizzas (p.87)

Cheese Gougères (p.97)

Pesto Star Bread (p.121)

Sura's Parsley, Feta and Spinach Turkish Pastries (p.210)

Sourdough (p.219)

Cheese and Spring Onion Scones (p.227)

Spinach, Fennel and Feta Galette (p.235)

Herby Garlic Rolls (p.241)

Index

This book is published to accompany the television series entitled *The Great British Baking Show* in the United States

This book is published to accompany the television series entitled *The Great British Bake Off*, broadcast on Channel 4 in 2020

The Great British Bake Off® is a registered trademark of Love Productions Ltd

Series produced for Channel 4 Television by Love Productions

First published in Great Britain in 2020 by Sphere

10 9 8 7 6 5 4 3 2 1

Text and recipes © Love Productions Ltd 2020
Design and recipe photography © Little, Brown Book Group 2020
Additional photography© Love Productions Ltd 2020

A CIP catalogue record for this book is available from the British Library.

ISBN 978-0-7515-8305-2

New recipes developed and written by: Annie Rigg and Lisa Sallis
Editorial Director: Hannah Boursnell
Commissioning Editor: Fiona Rose
Design & Art Direction: Smith & Gilmour
Project Editor: Judy Barratt
Copyeditor: Nicola Graimes
Editorial Assistant: Ruth Jones
Recipe Tester: Mitzie Wilson
Food Photographer: Jamie Orlando-Smith
On-set GBBO Photography: Mark Bourdillon
Food Stylist: Annie Rigg
Assistant Food Stylist: Lola Milne
Props Stylist: Cynthia Blackett
Production Manager: Abby Marshall
Cover Design: Smith & Gilmour

Publisher's thanks to: Susie Adam, Lexi Amedee, Jan Billington, Hilary Bird, Scott Chalmers, Joanna Clarke, Sarah Epton, Tammy Flavell, Lola Joshua, Jack Joshua, Serafina Lewis, Martha Limberg, Lola Milne, Arjun Singh Panam, Jude Sharkey, Lily Smith, Oscar Smith, Findlay Sokal, Talia Sokal, and (of course) Chewie the dog.

Typeset in Archer, Golden Plains and Gill Sans
Colour origination by Born Group
Printed and bound in Canada by Friesens.

Papers used by Sphere are from well-managed forest and other responsible sources.

Sphere
An imprint of Little, Brown Book Group, Carmelite House, 50 Victoria Embankment, London EC4Y 0DZ
An Hachette UK Company
www.hachette.co.uk www.littlebrown.co.uk

WITH THANKS

Love Productions would like to thank the following people:
Producer: Jenna Mansfield
Challenge Producer: Tallulah Radula-Scott
Food Producer: Katy Bigley
Home Economist: Becca Watson
Love Executives: Letty Kavanagh, Rupert Frisby, Kieran Smith, Joe Bartley
Publicists: Amanda Console, Shelagh Pymm
Commissioning Editors: Kelly Webb-Lamb, Sarah Lazenby

Thank you also to: Paul, Prue, Noel and Matt. *And to the bakers for their recipes:* Dave, Hermine, Laura, Linda, Loriea, Lottie, Makbul, Marc, Mark, Peter, Rowan and Sura.